NEW HORIZONS

Our Adventure
in the World of the Street

Chiara Amirante

NEW HORIZONS
Our Adventure
in the World of the Street

Introduction by Luigi Accattoli

Epilogue by Daniel-Ange

New City

London

First published as *Nuovi Orizzonti*
© 1996 by Città Nuova, Rome

First published in Great Britain 2009 by
New City
Unit 17, Sovereign Park
Coronation Road
London NW10 7QP

© 2009 English Translation New City London
Translated by Frank Johnson

Cover design Tomeu Mayans
Picture © Marilynv/Dreamstime.com

British Cataloguing in Publication Data:
A catalogue reference for this book is available from
the British Library

ISBN 978 1 905039 10 4

Typeset by New City, London
Printed and bound by Gutenberg Press Ltd, Tarxien, Malta

Contents

Introduction

I've never met Chiara Amirante, but I am happy that she lives in Rome and that she talks to the homeless at Termini railway station. If there is a woman, even just one, who does that, and if this Christian woman is 30, it means that all is not lost.

I live within a stone's throw of Stazione Termini and I've seen how the area has changed over the years, invaded by a random population of prostitutes, drug addicts and tramps.

My house is in Via Santa Maria Maggiore and when I worked for *Repubblica**, to get to Piazza Indipendenza I passed by Termini at all hours of the day and night. In the weeks when I was working nights, I would pass by at three in the morning.

I saw stabbings and police swoops. I saw the first bivouacs of the drug addicts and the first little groups of immigrants from the Third World who now are a large and permanent presence there. I saw the prostitutes who every year took over another 50 metres of Via Cavour and who now populate the pavements in front of my house, and there are Slavs and Africans and they all get together at any time like school friends.

I always asked myself: what would Jesus do, what

* an Italian daily newspaper

would St Francis or St Catherine do if they passed by these men and women? Now I know: they would do something similar to what Chiara is doing. Chiara hasn't come down from heaven and she didn't live in the Middle Ages. She is a Roman, with dark eyes and wavy hair and she says she was scared when she decided to follow this path: scared of telling her parents, because she was a girl and it could be dangerous!

I had already read the book *Stazione Termini* by Chiara Amirante – a story of drugs, AIDS and prostitution. And I had seen her on TV in 'inchieste di Biagi' (Biagi's Enquiries) on 28 October 1994. I dedicated one of the 224 stories in my own book *Cerco fatti di Vangelo* (Search for the Facts of the Gospel) in 1995. So, I knew something, but I have learnt much more from this little book, because here Chiara tells her story as it happened.

Everything happens in this girl's life. She is saved from a road accident and her best friend is killed, run over by a car. She goes through a dark night which she calls 'black-out'. She gets an eye disease which could make her blind. She is very ill for five years and then is suddenly healed.

So, having been tried in this way, she sets off on her adventure. Her genius is her roadside encounters. There is David who is dying of AIDS and John with his rucksack, his penny whistle and his dog: Chiara speaks to all of them about Jesus. She is present during exorcisms, she meets girls who become prostitutes in order to pay for their drugs, and those who take drugs to have the courage to become prostitutes. And, as if all this didn't affect her, she comes to us at the beginning of the book 'happy to be alive' and she bids us farewell happily, on the last page.

What is Chiara's secret? It is the simplest of all: to see her neighbour and to speak to him or her. And so, even a desolate place like Stazione Termini becomes the setting for a never-ending Christian adventure.

Luigi Accattoli

To the reader

Perhaps you too have sometimes heard disquieting questions knocking at the door of your soul. Perhaps you have resisted them in the vain hope of chasing them back into the secret depths of your most intimate self. Perhaps you have done this because they seem to threaten the precarious equilibrium you had achieved. But then, whenever you find the courage to stop for a moment, to extinguish the deafening noises of the world which disturb you, and finally to listen to the voice of silence, you rediscover those same questions waiting to ambush you: Who am I? Why do I exist? What is the meaning of life? Why is there so much suffering?

You will have felt a deep thirst for truth and you will have asked yourself which path you should follow to arrive finally at that spring able to satisfy your thirst. You will have pounded around in search of freedom, in the hope that one day you will find a way to break those mysterious chains which held you so firmly every time you tried to "break free". And you will have started asking, knocking, searching for something, or perhaps for Someone who can give answers to the secret needs of your spirit.

You will have followed many pathways, gathered many flowers along the road and discovered some precious pearls. And certainly, before each discovery, you will have leapt for joy and felt the desire to share your excitement, your surprise, with another.

So, I would like to try in these few pages to share with you, my companion on the journey, something of those new horizons which the Love of loves has given me to contemplate every time I wasn't afraid to abandon myself completely to Him, to let myself be led along His paths of light.

It's just an attempt. In fact, if you love the truth, you will know very well how difficult it is to find words adequate to describe His beauty, but I am sure that in your eagerness to discover, you will also be able to understand what words cannot express.

Why?

I feel a sense of wonder whenever I see children. I could spend hours looking at the beauty of their expressions, the lack of self-consciousness in their actions, their spontaneity. But what attracts me most of all about children is their capacity to ask questions about everything. Those thousands of questions which often to us adults, who like to think of ourselves as having "certainties", seem only annoying and exhausting, often contain great wisdom. I believe they are like a trampoline launching us on a journey into the infinite universe of the knowledge of truth. But too often the "wisdom" of "mature" persons who like to remain on the surface so as to maintain the illusion of certainty, silences the child, disguising their refusal to let the child's questions send them into crisis. Thus, gradually, the child starts to believe that, to appear intelligent in front of adults, he has to stop asking so many "useless" questions and pretend that he knows and understands everything. In this way he ends up not asking anything any more and learns from his elders to fool himself into believing he knows everything. He learns to be constantly bewildered by the thousands of "noises" of the world, while not having the time to listen to the many questions which remain unanswered because they have been liquidated, very diplomatically, by the adults. The child, in his simplicity, is not afraid to ask the reason why for everything he observes: Mummy, why does the sky exist? Why is Daddy always so nervous? Why is that little bird dead? Why does day come after night, followed by day again? Why do I have to go to school today? Why don't you play too? But the adult escapes, he is afraid of allowing himself to be penetrated by these threatening questions. He needs to have everything under control, to be in charge of everything around him and very rarely does he find the courage to explore the mysteries of things that are difficult to understand.

However, the child is disappointed by the adults' hurried and superficial replies and, when he feels he has really grown up and he too is certain about everything, unexpectedly the same old questions come to the surface again. But this time they do not come with the innocence and tranquillity of childhood; this time they are accompanied by a deep feeling of fear and of being lost. And he can continue to flee from the silence, blocking his ability to listen in a thousand ways so that he doesn't have to think (continuous chatting, hyperactivity, passions, thousands of imaginary problems, TV, sex, drugs, rock and roll...). Or he can decide to let himself enter into the intimacy of the questions and finally the "crisis" will arrive. I say finally, because I don't think one can grow without some sort of trial: there cannot be true knowledge without the courage to entrust oneself to the night of doubt and uncertainty.

And it is from the moment he starts not to be afraid of this crisis that life seems new and full of colour. And it is thanks to the pressing insistence of the questions of my childhood that today I feel so happy to live and am always more satisfied by truth. Because if, on the one hand, doubt leads you along the steep and narrow way of uncertainty

14

and fear, on the other hand it reveals to you new heavens of truth.

There are many questions that accompanied me from childhood and there are many answers that I have gathered on the path of life. I never grow tired of putting questions to myself and of exploring the world of truth, because truth is the Infinite itself.

When I was a little girl I used to love letting off steam with my friends in the garden, and the games I liked best were the most daring ones. I was certainly a very lively child and I loved being with others, but every so often I felt the need to be on my own to reflect a little. I would look up at the sky and just be fascinated by it; I would look at the flowers and try to distinguish their thousands of different shades, and I would ask myself where all this perfection and beauty came from. I would listen to the birds singing and the sound of the wind and I would try not to lose even a single note of the harmony of that concerto. Like all children, I never grew tired of asking myself and others the reason behind everything. But I thank my parents with all my heart for having listened to me patiently and for never having pretended to have an answer for everything. There were never nice, ready-made, "clear-cut" answers that would shut me up and reassure me. More often than not my Dad, in reply, posed other questions; mealtimes often turned into philosophi-cal-theological dissertations.

Perhaps, at that time, I would have been happy to have been given reassuring and superficial answers, to avoid the torment of doubt, but how grateful I am now to my parents for not having fobbed me off with made-up explanations! Often, it makes me smile when grown-ups say with great conviction: "But she is a child, she doesn't understand!" However, I still remember vividly the suffering I felt when I was five years old, when I couldn't find the answer to certain questions. Looking at nature I felt a strong desire to know the Author of such wonders and I asked myself what I had to do to be a note in that ineffable harmony. My intuition was that what my parents, who had recently become Christians, told me, that "God is love", was true, but I couldn't understand why there was so much evil, so much suffering, why it was so difficult to be good... and sometimes I was in tears because I couldn't fathom that mystery.

It's certainly not that I spent my childhood between one existential crisis and another: I liked to enjoy myself and most of the time I did. But my inability never to put aside those questions was very important in helping me be aware of my spiritual needs and of not neglecting them.

In fact, I believe that most of the suffering and the unhappiness of humanity today comes from the fact that we have chosen to ignore the reality that we are not just made of body and psyche, but also of spirit. And just as the body and the psyche have their needs and when these needs are not satisfied we can become ill, the same thing applies to the spirit. The consumerism and hedonism on which we feed ourselves want to convince us that it is enough to satisfy our need for pleasure, success, possessions, in order to be happy; and yet no society like our consumer and hedonist society has been so "successful" in producing so many depressions and suicides. We try in every way possible to avoid unhappiness, but still it pursues us, it follows us without leaving us alone for an instant. It is like a cancer that gradually spreads with all its metastases, and we never find the courage to tear it out.

On the other hand, if it is true that if we don't eat or sleep we become ill, it is also true that if we don't decide to feed our spirit nothing will be able to make us feel really well. So, it is essential to find the time for the child who is still clammering within us, to identify, thanks to his questions, some fundamental needs of our spirit and not to ignore them.

It is really thanks to these annoying and insistent questions of our childhood: Why do evil, suffering, anxiety, war, darkness, lies, slavery, death exist? Why does the world exist?... that I was able to understand how much my spirit needed goodness, love, peace, unity, light, truth, freedom, life...; I realised just how much we need He who created us!

But how can we respond to these needs? *I am the way, the truth and the life…"* (Jn 14: 6); *"ask and it will be given you, seek and you will find, knock and it will be opened to you"* (Lk 11: 9). The only thing left for me to do was to ask, to knock, to seek, in order to know and follow the way and the truth that lead to the life!

The Way

"In the beginning was the Word, and the Word was with God, and the Word was God. He was in the beginning with God. All things came into being through him, and without him not one thing came into being. What has come into being in him was life, and the life was the light of all people... And the Word became flesh and lived among us" (Jn 1: 1-4, 14).

What an ineffable mystery: He, through whom everything was made, becomes flesh in order to live among us! So, who better than He, who created us and wanted to become man to reveal his love to us, will be able to give an answer to the most intimate questions of my heart?

If the life is in Him and the life is the light of humanity, who better than the Word can teach me to live life to the full and illuminate the night of my doubts?

But *"The light shines in the darkness, and the darkness did not overcome it"* (Jn 1: 5). How can we avoid being immersed in the darkness that surrounds us? It would be terrible to find ourselves amongst those who did not want to accept the light.

These and a thousand other considerations led me to accept my parents' suggestion: "If you want to find answers, look for them in the Gospel. But don't study it like you would any other book; try rather to live it, because it contains words of life."

In fact, this was the great discovery that my parents had recently made thanks to their meeting the focolarini.

These focolarini were indeed very special people and I too was always very happy when they came to our house. Their infectious joy and their serenity made what they said believable: "God is love, God is joy, God is freedom and truth! If you live His word you too can experience 'the fullness of his joy'." I realised that in them the love, the joy and the freedom they spoke about were not just words, but a tangible reality in their lives. I was convinced by this and so I set off on the same path as them.

It really was a marvellous path and I went with growing enthusiasm from one discovery to another. Every time I met with other young people who had chosen to follow the same path it was cause for a great celebration. And in sharing the treasures we had discovered we had the feeling that they had been multiplied. Of course, it wasn't always a bed of roses. For one thing, my new friends lived in different towns and it wasn't easy to get together.

My school friends and playmates had chosen other, very different ways; the Gospel law of love can seem like madness compared to the laws of the world which are so deeply rooted in selfishness.

For me too it was a difficult task to free myself from the chains of selfishness which imprisoned me so firmly, but every time, by the grace of God, I was able to liberate myself, I experienced an extraordinary freedom and fullness.

It was exciting to discover that Christianity, although apparently in contrast with human logic, can reveal the secrets of interior light and transform a heart of stone into a heart overflowing with joy. The meeting with He who makes all things new works this miracle of rebirth. On the ruins of the demolished self a new life flourishes and we taste finally the elation of the flight into immensity: we experience the freedom of the children of God. And when we have touched the "heaven of love" we cry out our *eureka!* Yes, because our Creator impresses in our soul an agonising desire for "the things of above" and until we have had the chance to taste at least a drop of the Eternal, we have a bitter taste in our mouths. Always restless and unsatisfied, we return to the mirages of the world in a breathless race that exhausts us and makes us incapable of raising our eyes towards heaven.

If you too are one of those who has hoped for and pursued something that might quench the soul's thirst; if you too have experienced bitterness when following the dreams of the world; if you have been fooled by trying to satisfy your needs with yet another possession and each time you felt an even greater thirst; if you have ever felt lost and disorientated amidst the absurdities of a world which feeds itself on lies, you will certainly be able to understand the joy I felt when I was able to pronounce and then repeat with growing conviction my *eureka*, I have found it! Yes, I have found the way that leads to the truth; I have found the spring that can quench the thirst of my heart, I have found He who does not betray, but who pours a sweet balm on the wounds of my soul; I have found the answer in a God who loved me to the point where he wanted to "forget" his omniscient being to be alongside me and to cry out with me "Why?"

The Secret

What excitement! In a short while Chiara[1] would be arriving and we could hardly contain ourselves. We were gathered together from all over the world for our international Gen 3 congress[2]. I was only 11, but for me that meeting was unforgettable, because those words of light remained engraved on my heart in letters of fire, marking an important step.

Chiara had been welcomed, as always, by a real explosion of uncontrollable joy. We had prepared a lot of questions for her and her replies were listened to with a religious silence as they penetrated deep into our souls, dissipating every doubt. I was enraptured by the incredible light that she brought to us, and when she was asked to open her heart and tell us her secret, our emotions rose even higher. I had often asked myself what was the secret behind the fact that a simple girl like her had been able to bring to birth such a vast international movement. What was the secret that had enabled her to overcome with such strength and serenity the many crosses in her life and become an instrument of joy and light for so many.

[1] Chiara Lubich, founder of the Focolare Movement
[2] Boys and girls aged between 9 and 16, members of the Focolare Movement

And now it was she herself who was to reveal that secret to me; I was absolutely thunderstruck by it. It is impossible to explain what I experienced in those few moments. I had the feeling almost, that Jesus himself was giving me a new heart. It was no longer my mind, me as a person who was listening: *"Those who are unspiritual do not receive the gifts of God's Spirit, for they are foolishness to them"* (1 Cor 2:14): I had a heart of flesh capable of savouring the presence of God, and it was so moving that only those who have experienced it can understand it. Suddenly everything seemed clear in my heart... even the ineffable mystery of the cross! I was in the front row and I could see in Chiara's eyes the love of a creature completely in love with Jesus crucified and forsaken. And the love that vibrated between us and our hearts revealed something of the love contained in the cry: *"My God, my God, why have you forsaken me?"* (Mt 27: 46). The mystery of the love of God that takes upon himself our darkness to give us his Light, our anguish to give us his Peace, our suffering to give us his Joy, our weakness to make us strong in him, our separation from heaven to reunite us with the Father, our doubt to reveal to us that he is the Answer and the Truth, our death to let us experience the Resurrection, our hell to let us enter into the Paradise of life, with Him, through Him and in Him!

Chiara explained to us that for her every painful situation, every suffering neighbour no longer represented a meeting with suffering, but a chance to meet Jesus crucified and forsaken and that every suffering lived with Him and out of love for Him was transformed into that "grain of wheat which dies, yes, but in order to produce more fruit!"

The overwhelming truth proclaimed by St Paul: *"He has given his life for me"* (Gal 2: 20), struck my "new heart" like a fiery dart and my spirit experienced a feeling of dizziness. I recollected myself for a moment in the intimate tabernacle of my soul, moved and overcome in the contemplation of that ineffable reality: "You God, the Eternal, the Absolute, the Immense, the Omnipotent, the beauty of all beauties, the light of every light, you have loved me to the point of taking up all my suffering so that I can see your infinite love! You have loved me to the point of dying on the cross for me, so that I could know the fullness of life that is in you!" "He gave his life for me!" (cf. Gal 2: 20) The ABC of Christianity, in which I had always believed, was for me, in that moment, an overwhelming revelation. I had the sensation that a divine bomb had exploded inside me, setting fire to the whole of my being with a fire of love. So, for me, the obvious thing to do was immediately to draw the conclusion: "But you who are God, the Creator, the Infinite One, wanted to give your life for me who am nothing, a miserable sinner, how can I now not give my life for you, how can I now not live to say thank you?"

The mass which took place straight after the meeting with Chiara was a chance to consecrate my life to God. It was a very solemn moment, and if on the one hand my heart was overflowing with joy, on the other I was only too aware that I was choosing to repeat with St Paul: *"For I decided to know nothing among you except Jesus Christ, and him crucified"* (1 Cor 2: 2); I was choosing to remain nailed to those two pieces of wood with Jesus, I was deciding to follow "the narrow way of the cross" without ever looking back. My tears were streaming down, but I was happy because I knew

I was choosing to follow the Love of loves and, following the way prepared for me from all Eternity, I would contemplate all his wonders. I asked for the grace to be faithful to this consecration and felt reborn; I felt as if I was flying!

Back in my home town – I was living in Brindisi at the time – I felt a very strong desire to tell my friends all that had happened.

I couldn't wait to shout it out to everyone, but I didn't know how to.

How could I explain the inexplicable: the encounter with the overwhelming and regenerating Power of the love of God? Our words are finite, limited, they can't recount the experience of the Infinite! But I didn't give up: the others had to know this, and so I invented all sorts of things so that I could share my enthusiasm for my discovery. And many understood…

We had one huge factor in our favour: we were still children and we couldn't pack the Immense into our own little mental categories, where it would never have fitted! We liked simplicity, and He who is simple loves to hide Himself from the wise so that he can reveal himself to the little ones: "Whoever does not receive the kingdom of God as little child will never enter it" (cf. Mk 10: 15).

That's how we started, with a few friends, meeting from time to time to deepen our understanding of that passage.

Pearls of Light

In every word of the Gospel I saw a pearl of incandescent light and I never tired of drawing on that inexhaustible well.

I had also sought joy, and now the meeting with He who is truth stripped bare the thousands of lies that had weighed down my life up till then.

I saw the people around me busying themselves in pursuit of "idols": money, success, power. But the more they had the more they wanted, the more they affirmed themselves the more they wanted to affirm themselves. They were busily chasing the mirage of happiness, trampling on everything and everybody in the process, without ever obtaining it. I, on the other hand, was discovering, in the logic of Christianity which is so illogical to the world, the way of joy: *"As the Father has loved me, so have I loved you. Now remain in my love. If you obey my commands, you will remain in my love, just as I have obeyed my Father's commands and remain in his love. I have told you this so that my joy may be in you and that your joy may be complete"* (Jn 15: 9-11). "My command is this: Love each other as I have loved you. Greater love has no-one than this that he lay down his life for his friends" (Jn 15 12-13). It had all become clear, the lie had been unmasked.

The world taught me that I had to feel as if I where the centre of the universe and to use things and people to achieve my aims. I needn't worry about the person next to me, but only about my personal fulfilment.

My Creator, on the other hand, who knew the secret needs of my heart more than anyone else, was saying exactly the opposite to me: "Forget yourself and love! Don't be suffocated by your selfishness, but be ready to give your life for your friends; then, and only then, will your joy be full! You must be ready to lose your life if you want to save it: you have to deny yourself, renounce the tyranny of your self if, finally, you want to feel free in joy." Certainly, to renounce the tyranny of myself was no small thing; but in this way I could be sure that my Creator really wasn't mistaken and that his commandments were not prohibitions and limitations, but advice from a heavenly Father who, loving his children infinitely, wants nothing other than their happiness.

So, it was a question of making a choice: allow myself to be led by the desires of the flesh, as the world continuously suggests to us, or decide to walk according to the Spirit, in order to savour the fruits of peace, joy and love. The truth of the word of God was very clear, it did not leave any room for doubt: *"So I say, live by the Spirit, and you will not gratify the desires of the sinful nature. For the sinful nature desires what is contrary to the Spirit, and the Spirit what is contrary to the sinful nature. They are in conflict with each other, so that you do not do what you want [...] The acts of the sinful nature are obvious: sexual immorality, impurity and debauchery; idolatry and witchcraft; hatred, discord, jealousy, fits of rage, selfish ambition, dissensions, factions and envy; drunkenness, orgies, and the like. I warn you, as I did before, that those who live like this will not inherit the kingdom of God. But the fruit of the Spirit is love, joy, peace, patience, kindness, goodness, faithfulness, gentleness and self-control"* (Gal 5: 16-17, 19-22).

The hedonist mentality wants us to believe that we have to satisfy the desires of the flesh in order to be happy, while the word of God tells us that these desires preclude us from the kingdom of God and do not allow us to savour the fruits of the Spirit: peace, joy and love, of which we have need. I realised that following passions, instincts, moods, things I "like" or "don't like", is much easier than listening to our conscience. The requests of the Spirit are demanding and require a certain effort, destroying is much easier than building; but what a delusion to find oneself with nothing but ruins in one's hands, and what satisfaction if we can build works which have solid foundations! *"A man reaps what he sows. The one who sows to please his sinful nature, from that nature will reap destruction; the one who sows to please the Spirit, from the Spirit will reap eternal life"*(Gal 6:7-8).

The only thing I could do therefore, was to sow in the Spirit and learn that difficult but most precious art which is prayer; I had to give up following my own ways, so that I could be led in His: *"For my thoughts are not your thoughts, neither are your ways my ways"* (Is 55: 8).

For someone as stubborn as me, who always wants to do things off my own bat, it was not an easy school: I had difficulty abandoning myself completely to the works of the heavenly Father and offered resistance with my continuous reasoning. Fortunately I had never completely given up the childlike simplicity which is always there within us and this helped me learn the art of listening to my conscience. Every time the heart overcame the head and I threw myself freely into the arms of the Father, I experienced an incredible joy and every moment was new and full of surprises.

Walking along the pathways of love I experienced life as an extraordinary, divine adventure.

Everything interested me and seemed beautiful. I liked to stop and listen to the mysterious notes of silence which, together with the song of nature, composed a marvellous symphony – the sweetest music that spoke to me of majesty, of beauty, and of the love of my Creator.

The encounter with every person that passed by me excited me, because I tried to capture, beyond the mask, the inestimable treasures imprinted by the Creator in each of his creatures.

I was passionate about any situation or activity during the day, because every little thing lived in love acquired a value and was an opportunity to learn and discover something new.

I had always dreamt of freedom and finally, thanks to prayer, which gives the spirit wings to fly into immensity, I felt free of any conditioning, prejudices, conventions, labels, masks and passions.

I savoured the beauty of the freedom that comes from Spirit and not from the flesh. "The truth will make you free." Making myself live in the truth, to live the word of God who is Truth, finally the chains of passions, impulses, pride and sin which imprisoned me were broken. I then saw just how illusory was the freedom proclaimed by hedonism. There is a saying: "To be free you have to give free rein to your instincts, you must always do what you want to do without worrying about anything else!" And everyone seems so convinced by this that you end up believing it too and falling into the trap. You let yourself be seduced by so many illusions. You let yourself be caught up in the illusion of false freedom and then you find yourself increasingly a slave: of your passions, of your need to please others and your need to receive support and reward, dependent on everyone and everything (on sex, on drugs, on other people). It feels as if you've landed in a swamp you can't get out of and your anguish increases. So it seemed like a dream that I had met someone who was able to break my chains with the "sword" of truth and drag me out of the swamp.

Finally, opening my heart to the love of God, I tasted interior peace and could see clearly that anguish is a disease of the spirit.

If we fail to draw on the well of peace and follow the steep and rugged paths of prayer, sooner or later our spirit will find itself in agony. If we refuse to listen to our conscience which, very discreetly, always tells us the right thing to do, certainly the vice-like grip of our sense of guilt will not slacken and our attempts to close our ears, to anaesthetise our unhappy interior, will not succeed in uprooting the evil of anguish.

"Peace I leave with you; my peace I give you. I do not give to you as the world gives" (Jn 14: 27).

Only the encounter with He who is peace can heal the many wounds which sin has inflicted on our spirit and remove the cancer of anguish.

Only Love Remains

I just about had time to realise that we had gone off the road and that the car was hanging over the edge of a steep drop. But that moment seemed like an eternity. A charge of fear ran through my body like an electric shock and thousands of chaotic thoughts came flooding into my mind in a fraction of a second: "It's not possible, is it already finished? What will remain of my life?"

Anyone who has faced death knows very well that it is not a pleasant experience and that the natural reaction is to want to run away from it at any cost. Thanks be to God, death did not manage to take us, also because we did our best to escape it. An adrenaline rush made us scramble out of the car before it was too late.

I was still a bit afraid and disorientated when I realised that we were out of danger. At Sperlonga, Francesco, when he and Aldo left the group, had had one glass of wine too many and he had lost control of the car on the badly-lit road. Judging by the damage to the car, we were lucky to be alive, but fortunately we got away with just a few scratches.

At that time of night the road was not very busy and so we had to wait a while before help arrived.

Eventually the rest of our party arrived. Having lost sight of us they had turned back to see what had happened. When they found us they were already panicking and crying because before they saw us, they saw the state of the car at the bottom of the drop and thought we were dead, or at least gravely injured. It took a while for us to reassure them that we were all alive and that, apart from a few scratches and bruises, we were OK.

The incident was quite upsetting for all of us and we stopped there talking about it for some time.

We were on holiday at Terracina, guests of a friend, and I was sharing a room with Claudia and Daniela. After the accident we couldn't get to sleep, so we spent the rest of the night talking about and reflecting on death.

I had often reflected on the fact that one of the few certainties we have is that we will die. But when you find yourself facing death it is completely different. I was in shock and felt disorientated, but I also felt a great joy because I knew I still had some time left to live. I confided in Claudia that just before jumping out of the car I had felt a very strong certainty: *"Only love remains!"* Yes, I had felt a great suffering at the thought that my life had already reached the end of the line – the suffering of having loved too little.

It's true that we only appreciate the value of what we have when we are about to lose it. Faced with death I realised as never before, the immense gift that is life; so, what could I do so as not to arrive at the moment of death with the suffering of having wasted this gift?

I continued to chat to Claudia and Daniela, trying to penetrate the mystery of death and of life, until we decided to make a pact: we committed ourselves to help one another not to waste even an instant of our lives, trying to live with intensity and with love, to be ready when the moment of passing to the other life arrived.

This pact calmed us and finally we fell into a deep sleep. The encounter with death and our pact left a deep mark on us and in the days that followed we took every opportunity to communicate our discoveries to each other, to share the fruits of our meditations and the difficulties and to give us new strength to go ahead on the adventure of love.

Four months later, unexpected news. It hit me like a cold shower as I was going down the stairs in church. I understood from Sandra's trembling voice that it was something serious: "Chiara," she said, "do you know what happened yesterday? While Claudia was on her way home she was crossing the road when a drunken driver shot out suddenly like a madman and hit her full on! Now she is in hospital, in a coma, but there isn't much hope... I'm sorry I am the one to give you this terrible news."

It felt as if my heart had been pierced, I couldn't believe it: Claudia in a coma? I had seen her just a few days before, full of life, and that very afternoon I had arranged to go and see her to tell her some really beautiful things. I didn't even get the chance to see her: a few hours later Claudia died.

It is impossible to describe what you go through when you are told that someone you loved dearly has died suddenly. If I hadn't been comforted by the certainty that we would meet again in heaven, I would have felt completely crushed by the weight of suffering and incapable of getting up again.

I was deeply shocked and even though I carried on with my normal life, I saw everything with different eyes.

I looked at the world around me and suddenly everything seemed absurd. The streets crowded with people who, as ever, were rushing about here and there; my friends worried about their exams; the television with its usual adverts and programmes like Dallas which want you to drink in that what counts in life is money, success, power... whereas you have been hit by the reality of death which smacks you in the face with one single truth: everything is vanity of vanities! What is the point of running after money, a career, material goods, if none of it remains, given that the "millstone of death" will inevitably reduce it all to dust?

I roamed around the streets like a battered dog that can't find refuge or consolation anywhere; all the rushing around that I could see seemed to be a complete non-sense.

My wounded heart kept repeating: "Claudia, where are you? Why did you leave me? We could have spent so many beautiful and important moments together. Why are you dead?" But it was as if the word "dead" was dying on my lips. No, Claudia was not dead, she had simply passed on to a new life, to that eternal life where, sooner or later, I too would join her. And it was as if she continued repeating to me: "Everything passes, everything passes, only love remains." In this way, the pact with which we had promised to help each other to live life with intensity, in love, through love and for love, to prepare ourselves for the day of the big meeting with He who is Love, became more sacred than ever for me: it had been sealed by her very own life.

The Crossroads

The impact with university life was not great. Gradually I managed to get used to the anonymity of the great metropolis, but going into lecture theatres with two or three hundred people where each one was like an island, after having lived a special harmony with my school friends, was neither simple nor pleasant. Fortunately, in political science I had a group of friends who always met together, but most of the young people I met gave me the impression of being alone and disorientated in the midst of that crowd. There were a lot of "outsiders", young people who had come to Rome from other towns to go to university and who found it difficult to settle in. Speaking with some of my friends, we had an idea: why not open a study room that was a witness against the individualism that reigned supreme? A place where anyone who went would feel welcomed and could enjoy a family atmosphere? We would keep it open also at meal times, so that the outsiders would have somewhere to go when the other rooms were normally closed… Four of us rolled up our sleeves to prepare as best we could the places that had been allocated to us in the crypt of the university chapel. We organised an opening party to which more than two hundred students came. It was a chance to launch our proposal: oppose individualism and indifference with the strength of solidarity, friendship and love. Many gave their support immediately and so our room was opened straightaway. In a short time a group of more than three hundred young people was formed. We organised shifts: the "shift workers", two at a time, had to welcome whoever came to study in the room, to organise the tea and biscuits, which would be a chance for people to get to know one another and to share, and finally they would tell them about the various initiatives which from time to time would be launched.

A group of about 40 of us started to organise meetings to go into depth in the Gospel and to take the revolution of love into that environment. Every occasion was a good one: putting in common textbooks to help those who had financial difficulties; organising concerts for solidarity, trips out, shows, photographic exhibitions, study groups, debates… everything became a good opportunity to share with as many young people as possible the beauty of a life renewed by the Gospel.

Many were really struck by what they had discovered together and their enthusiasm brought in others. A considerable commitment of time and energy was required to follow the growing number of young people and the numerous activities, but I didn't feel it as a burden because the chance of sharing the extraordinary reality offered by Jesus: *"Where two or three come together in my name, there am I with them"* (Mt 18: 20) gave me such joy.

But just when I least expected it, I was struck by a disorienting black-out and I found myself in the deepest darkness. The light, the joy and the peace which up until that moment had filled my heart to overflowing, suddenly vanished, leaving my soul in the dark, in suffering and anguish. I couldn't understand what was happening to me. It was as if I had suddenly been catapulted into a vast desert, unable to find the well from which, until a short time ago, I had drawn in abundance.

I didn't feel communion with God any more, something which, until that moment, had coloured every instant of my life; every certainty had been wiped out in one move. It was as if all the beauty, all the life of the Spirit that I had lived in the past had disappeared, leaving me with the doubt that all I had had was a beautiful dream, an illusion. It was as if my heart had turned to stone and the senses of the spirit had been extinguished. I felt nothing but the weight of my limitations, of my littleness, of my misery; I thought that my sinfulness would exclude me forever from the extraordinary experience of paradise, of communion with He who is Love. God-Love was the ideal towards which I had directed my existence, he had been the breath of my life and now I felt mysteriously distant from him, incapable of feeling His presence in any way. What a suffering then, to discover that I even doubted His existence! I continued searching for Him, but even prayer had become a source of suffering: in fact, I felt like someone dying of thirst who doesn't know what to do to find water. Around me absolutely nothing had changed, but inside everything had: I felt I was dying, there was no longer that incredible fullness of life which previously I could not help but communicate to the people I met. It was by now a total crisis. The answers I had found in the past to my thousands of questions didn't exist any more and all I could do was to shout out: "My God, my God, why have you forsaken me?"

I found myself at a crossroads: to continue living according to the "absurd" logic of the Gospel, believing without seeing, or to let myself be carried along by the world and suffocate my spiritual needs, anaesthetising the terrible pain of the crisis with the thousands of options ready to hand which the consumer society was offering?

A very dear friend, who had always helped me a great deal, told me to believe that even the trial I was living was a sign of God's love and that behind my darkness there was the loving hand of the Father. Then she gave me something written by Chiara Lubich which speaks of the divine comedy. This made me reflect a lot: "Every time you feel despair in your soul and you continue smiling and talking about hope to the others [...] remember: that is the divine comedy."

I no longer had any certainties – not even that God existed, but of one thing I was sure: Rinata, my friend, loved me to the point that she was ready to give her life for me; so, if she asked me to believe without seeing, I had to do it. I decided to grit my teeth and set off on the "way of the divine comedy". They were painful but very precious months and when, at the end of the tunnel, the love of God gave me the grace once again to contemplate "His amazing light", I experienced an uncontainable joy.

Then, at that moment, having passed through the darkness, the doubt and the anguish and through the separation from God, I was able to enjoy, with such fullness, the beauty of His light, of the truth, the peace and the paradise that is communion with Him.

Two certainties remained imprinted on my soul after this experience: that there is no greater suffering than non-communion with God, because our soul has a very deep thirst for peace, joy and love, and He is the source of all this; that the only arrow capable of piercing a "heart of stone", which can't feel the presence of God, is love – the love that Jesus taught us and its measure which is to be ready to give our life for our friends (cf. Jn 15: 12-13). When the Word became flesh, although he could have chosen to do anything, not for nothing did he choose to die on the cross for us, and in taking our death upon himself, our separation from the Father, he gave us his own life and reunited us with the Father.

A Precious Crucible

"The zeal for your house devours me": after much suffering and wandering in my desert, love finally led me back to the spring. What joy to be able to draw abundantly on its water again!

I felt a fire burning within me that I could not contain. I had to return to the desert to tell my brothers and sisters who were "dying of thirst" that I had found the spring of living water again where they too could quench their thirst. But how could I convince them that they too could go to the fountain? Through love of course: *"My command is this: Love each other as I have loved you. Greater love has no-one than this, that he lay down his life for his friends"* (Jn 15: 12-13); a love ready to give its life for its neighbour: *"If we love one another, God lives in us and his love is made complete in us"* (1 Jn 4: 12).

It was this love that had convinced me and had allowed me to return to the spring. Opportunities to show this were certainly not lacking; many of the young people who came to our study room at the university confided their problems to us: crises, depressions, suicidal thoughts; their thirst and the search for something that would truly give meaning to their life. It was a joy to be able to "die and rise" with each one. The desire to share with as many people as possible the treasure I had finally discovered was such that I didn't realise that continuing to want to give my life for everyone I was forgetting that I also had to love myself: *"Love your neighbour as yourself"* (Mk 12: 31). I was working at breakneck speed: I would work into the wee small hours and during the day I had a thousand commitments and activities. Such was my enthusiasm that I ignored the repeated S.O.Ss from my own body as it pleaded for a moment's rest: continuous and very strong headaches and stomach aches, muscle weakness, fainting and insomnia. All this continued until my body, having tried everything, without success, to make me slow down, decided to go on strike; the result was a serious physical collapse. For a year or so I had a continuous slight temperature which didn't augur well either. One morning I awoke at around four in the morning with a piercing pain in one eye: it was as if someone has thrust a blade into it, with no way of pulling it out.

I went to see a doctor as soon as possible and was diagnosed with simple conjunctivitis. He didn't explain to me why simple conjunctivitis could cause such terrible pain, but I tried my best to live with it. After a week of Calvary, the pain, far from diminishing, had also struck the other eye; I decided to consult another doctor. While I was in the accident and emergency department having my eye looked at, the eye specialist could not hide his concern: "But how did you manage to put up with this pain for a week? It's not conjunctivitis; it's a serious case of uveitis. The infection has progressed a lot, has affected both eyes and has blocked the pupils. You risk losing your sight. We'll have to treat it immediately with cortisone and do a precise investigation to find the cause of the infection, because yours is a complex case."

This was a real blow for me. The doctor explained to me that in order to clear up the infection it would be necessary to treat the cause, but I would have to take the cortisone to avoid serious damage to my eyesight; this would then falsify to some extent the results of the investigation making it difficult to establish the cause of the infection. The result of the investigation was anything but reassuring. For a month I was subjected to a massive dose of antibiotics which in the end didn't achieve anything. The situation continued to worsen until they decided I needed to go into hospital. In hospital for a month, I underwent the most sophisticated of "Chinese tortures". There was a whole series of long "scopes" due to the inflammation that was attacking the respiratory, gastrointestinal and genital organs and on which anaesthetics had no effect. In fact, the pain, which had spread all over my body, was getting worse, not better. Added to this were the cortisone injections in the eyes which I had every other day and which were my "passion". After a broncoscopy which lasted three quarters of an hour without anaesthetic, they gave me the diagnosis: "It is chronic anterior uveitis which could eventually lead to blindness (I had already lost 80% of my vision); also there is a strong suspicion of Bechet's Syndrome (an incurable illness which no one would wish on their worst enemy) which we can only confirm over time."

My blood ran cold. What makes suffering tolerable is the fact that sooner or later it will come to an end: to hear them say that the eye disease was chronic and that I would eventually lose my sight was like being hit on the head.

For a moment, that peace which had incredibly stayed with me despite the lack of vision and the acute pain, abandoned me. I could do no more than cry out with all my soul: "Why Father, why have you allowed this? Couldn't you at least have let me die? How can I put up with all this suffering, for years maybe? And then what about my eyesight? Not being able to see any more? It will be terrible, I won't be able to do anything any more! I cannot believe it! Why, Father? Why?"

I went immediately to the chapel, my soul tormented by these thoughts, and while I was repeating this: "Why, Father?" There was someone reading a passage from Scripture out loud: "*Say to those with fearful hearts, Be strong, do not fear; your God will come [...] he will come to save you. Then will the eyes of the blind be opened and the ears of the deaf unstopped. Then will the lame leap like a deer, and the mute tongue shout for joy. Water will gush forth in the wilderness and streams in the desert [...] Gladness and joy will overtake them, and sorrow and sighing will flee away*" (Is 35: 4-6, 10). Those words entered my soul like a lance. Although in that moment the last thing I was thinking about was the possibility that I might regain my sight, I started to "see" spiritually and to believe that "everything works together for the good of those who love God". I felt enveloped by the love of the Father who gives courage to his children in moments of discomfort and a great peace returned within me that never left me. I just couldn't believe it. In theory at least, martyred by strong and incessant physical suffering and with a future that was far from rosy, I should have been desperate, but in fact I continued to experience an indescribable inner serenity and joy. I spent hours in prayer without tiring and, although nailed to the cross, with Him it seemed as if I was having a foretaste of a little bit of Paradise. I intuited something of the unfathomable mystery of suffering, I experienced just how much the cross can root us in the Essential and, if lived in love, how it can open up ever new horizons. On the other hand, if the Word incarnate chose the way of the cross, he will have had his own good reasons, he will have wanted us to grasp how precious it is, albeit difficult to understand.

Total trust in the love of God who *"disciplines those he loves, and punishes everyone he accepts as a son"* (Heb 12: 6), transformed my Calvary into a divine crucible. *"My child, when you come to serve the Lord, prepare yourself for testing [...] Accept whatever befalls you and in times of suffering be patient, for gold is tested in the fire and those found acceptable, in the crucible of suffering"* (Sir 2: 1, 4).

The fire of suffering was passing through me to burn all that is not God, to refine the gold and to bring light amidst the darkness. New fruits of a mysterious and profound joy were flowering on the death of that seed. I never failed to be amazed by this miracle: I was crucified with Christ, and yet I felt pervaded by the feast of the Resurrection. I wanted to sing out my joy to everyone and often, especially in the moments of deep prayer, I felt a strong urge to seek out all my friends who were immersed in despair, in drugs, in AIDS, in prostitution, to share my great discovery with them: every suffering lived with God is transformed into fire which refines the gold imprinted in us by the Creator, which warms the heart frozen by selfishness and brings light, peace and joy!

I realised that words could not express and explain the mysteries of love. They can only be intuited when you are experiencing them and it is love itself that reveals them to us. But the imperative *"Freely you have received, freely give"* (Mt 10: 8) was becoming more and more pressing. I

47

knew very well that if I hadn't received love freely from certain people who were able to communicate to me with their lives the love of God, Truth, His light and joy, I too would have lived through suffering in desperation and not in Paradise. I realised too that the worst sufferings are not physical ones (I had reached record levels of that, but was living in joy), but rather spiritual ones: *"the wages of sin is death"* (Rm 6: 23). In the past I had suffered the agony of the soul separated from the Father when, because of the separation brought about by our sins, we can no longer draw on that unique "spring of living water" which quenches the thirst of our spirit. I understood now as never before why *"There will be more rejoicing in heaven over one sinner who repents than over ninety-nine righteous persons"* (Lk 15: 7).

Anyway I realised that my idea of going to the station and round the streets in the evenings looking for my brothers and sisters in despair, on drugs, in prostitution, in anguish, in "death", was not very wise: there were many genuine difficulties and plenty of good reasons against. But instead of going away, this idea came back to me even more strongly. I thought: "But you who are God wanted to leave heaven to become human like us; you wanted to take our death on yourself to give us your life; and you wanted to descend into hell to bring us Paradise; what should prevent me from following you in all this and for all of this? To descend with you and for you into the hell of so many of my brothers and sisters, so that your love can give them an intuition of the Paradise that you are."

I issued a kind of "challenge" to Jesus in order to understand what I should do: "I don't know if my slightly crazy desire to go to the station at night has been put in my heart by You, or if I am just losing it a bit because of my illness. I know that there are many spiritual and human dangers, but I also know that 'Everything is possible in He who gives me the strength', when I abandon myself to Your will. So I am signing a blank cheque, which is my yes to everything you want to ask of me. But I am also asking You to give me a sign, to see if my desire to seek out my brothers and sisters who live in the 'hell of the streets' and to take love to those who don't know it, comes from You. In my current physical state I couldn't do it even if I wanted to. So, if it is You who are giving me this desire, you will have to give me back a bit of health, at least the minimum necessary to let me do it."

Having already had dealings with the Omnipotent, I knew that I could expect anything from him, but once again His love left me speechless. To my great surprise I awoke the next day to find myself, after years of ill health, feeling fully fit. It seemed so incredible, that it took me days to believe it; it was a gift that was too beautiful and unexpected. I had been suffering for five years with chronic headaches and stomach aches, muscle weakness, nausea, fainting and insomnia and for a year I had a continuous temperature and inflammations and the results of the blood tests were quite worrying.

Also, for seven months my uveitis passed from one acute phase to another and the 80% vision I had lost didn't permit me either to read or write. All the many treatments prescribed by the doctors from the day I started to be unwell were completely useless, to the extent that two months previously I had decided not to take any more medicines. And, suddenly, it had all gone, as if I was waking up after a nightmare: the headache and the stomach ache had gone, my temperature was normal, I felt strong once more, the test results were normal and… to cap it all, even the uveitis had disappeared and my sight was perfect again! I really was healed! It was such a *shock* that I almost died of a heart attack when the eye specialist told me that the uveitis had gone. My doctor commented: "For anyone who doesn't believe, it's a mystery. For those who believe – it's a miracle. As far as I am concerned, if you want to find a plausible explanation for your illness and healing you should read Job."

To have my health back finally, after years of Calvary, was like a dream and I couldn't help but attribute it to the Omnipotent and to the little challenge I had put down the day before.

Street Hell

There was still a problem that was not easy to resolve: how to begin my "journey in the world of the street" without my parents dying with worry or having a heart attack. I knew very well that for parents the thought of their daughter going to the main railway station late at night to spend hours with young people who where hardly respectable was not a nice one. I really wanted to avoid making them into martyrs. They had already suffered enough because of my illness and it didn't seem right to inflict another heavy cross on them. In the end I managed to find a satisfactory "escape route". In July I was going to graduate with a degree in international political science: what better solution than to go for three months to Ireland, where I had some friends, with the excuse, to some extent true, of improving my English? There, in the evening, I would easily be able to visit my street friends without worrying my parents. Certainly, the idea of starting my new experience of the world of the street in a country where I didn't even speak the language very well made it all seem even more crazy, but I thought: "OK, it doesn't really follow the rules of logic, but what is logical about an omnipotent Creator who becomes man and is crucified for our sins? What is logical about a God who makes himself into bread in order to feed us? But if God loved us so madly, we could also be a bit mad for Him! We could put aside all our reasoning to follow His illogical logic. On the other hand, the Word of God assures me that: *'When I am weak, then I am strong'* (2 Cor 12: 10), because His power is manifested in our weakness; so, I was on the right track. I can't speak much English, I don't know anything about the geography of Dublin or Irish culture and customs, I can't count fully on my health yet (because, according to the doctors, just as my health returned so incredibly mysteriously, it could go again at any moment and I could be just as ill as before); but exactly because I can't count on anything other than my weakness, I can hope in His strength."

My parents were happy about my idea of going to Dublin and in August I found myself in a lovely little two-storey house in Dublin, welcomed by the warm smiles of Catherine, Moreith and Norma. And although my English left a lot to be desired, I was able to communicate easily and whenever words failed me, we resorted to miming. I spent the first few days getting used to my new surroundings, practising the language and finding out more about the "rough" parts of the city and the existing social structures. Then taking my courage in both hands to overcome any remaining fear, I decided to set off on my journey through the world of the street. As I got on the bus I was tormented by thousands of thoughts: "But where are you going? It's dangerous to go near certain types of people! And then, what are you going to say to them? Forget it – it's absurd. You can't do anything if so many choose to take drugs, become prostitutes, or drown their troubles with alcohol…"

However, I had no time to let these thoughts convince me to change my mind because immediately a young man, who was clearly a bit groggy, sat next to me. He had a bottle of beer in his hand and, without even asking him, he started to tell me the story of his alcoholism. He was a really nice lad, with a cheeky sort of face, who seemed to know what he was doing.

"Look at the weather!" he said to me, "First it's sunny and then it starts raining. It was supposed to have been a nice day and now it's gone all cloudy again! Here it's always raining. No wonder people drink: what else can you do?"

The fact that he drank a bit too much was certainly no mystery, considering the slurred way he spoke and the reek of alcohol that you could smell from three metres away. Nevertheless, it surprised me that such a young lad – he was probably about 24 and seemed reasonably bright – could be so drunk so early in the morning.

"I don't believe," I replied, "that someone like you can't find anything better to do than drink. There are many more interesting things to do."

"More interesting? I can't find anything to interest me. Everything bores me, even drinking. But with alcohol life seems a bit more bearable."

"Don't you have a job or some friends, something to fill up your day a bit?"

"A job, friends? Do you think it's easy for someone who has lived on the streets for 15 years, struggling to survive, to find a job? Here in Dublin not even young people with degrees can find jobs; so how do you think I can get one? I didn't even finish primary school! I tried for a long time, but apart from 'black' work where I was just totally exploited, I couldn't find anything. Friends... yes, I have plenty and none. I know lots of people, but the street is a jungle where you always have to fight if you don't want to be stabbed in the back."

"But why did you decide to live on the streets?"

"It wasn't me who decided. I just found myself there. My father is an alcoholic and my mother, to keep us, had to work away from home all day. There are seven children. Often, when my father came home he would beat my mother. Mammy put up with that life of hell for a few years and then she too started drinking. We were all small, we were hungry and we were scared of our father who was very violent. So we spent our days on the streets where we had to learn to be at war with the world and look after ourselves. If you live on the streets you have to belong to a gang and make others respect you through strength. Smoking, hash and alcohol are the daily bread and you go from one crime to another, trying to show the others that you are the strongest. My brother couldn't put up with this style of life for long: when he was 16 he committed suicide. I'm too much of a coward, too afraid of death, so I looked for consolation in alcohol. It helps keep me happy...

You're a nice girl, I'd like to stop and talk to you, but I've got to get off the bus here, I've got an appointment with someone. You couldn't leave me your phone number? I'd like to speak to you again."

"I'm sorry, but I don't have a phone number to give you, but I hope we manage to meet up again some time and continue our chat."

"I hope so too. Bye."

I was very struck by this encounter and by the ease with which this lad, whom I'd never set eyes on before, told me something about his life. Often we make judgements from the outside, but when we have the chance to enter into the drama which has made a young man, full of potential, a thief and an alcoholic, it becomes very difficult to "throw the first stone". I was deeply touched by his sadness and immediately took a liking to him. In the days that followed I remembered him often, also in my prayers. I asked He who is the light to illuminate with His ray the darkness of non sense, so that my new friend could soon experience the joy of living.

I got off the bus at a stop near a small centre for the homeless. I felt certain that there I would meet someone who needed help. In fact, hardly had I crossed the threshold than I was stopped by Jean, a vagabond in the world, who confided his worries to me as if he had always known me. He had a huge desire to have his little "princess" with him again. In fact, his daughter had been taken from him because of his vagrancy and he couldn't find any peace until he had her with him again. He had been wondering aimlessly from town to town for years, jobless. His daughter, Clare, was the only one who could give any meaning or colour to his life, and he had no intention of just letting her go. To know that she had been entrusted to another family who would never, but never, be able to love her like he did, was a cause of great suffering.

Then I met David. He was squatting on a step and asking passers-by for money. His eyes were fixed on the pavement with his head resting on the gate behind the steps. He looked disconsolate. I didn't have much in my pocket, as I was used to going round with just a bit of loose change, but I was happy to give it to him.

"I'm sorry," I said, "that's all I've got, but it's better than nothing!"

He raised his head, completely taken aback and, thanking me, he gave me a beautiful smile. He had a young face, which was rather drawn, and he looked in a pretty bad state.

"Could I help you at all?" I said in my rather broken English, "You seem very sad to me?"

"You're right, I am sad! I feel almost desperate. If only someone could help me! Unfortunately there is no one who can help me any more. I have been condemned to death with no chance of the sentence being commuted!"

"Desperate? Condemned to death?" I repeated with a tone of voice clearly intended to provoke a response from David.

"For about a year," he explained, "thanks to a rehabilitation centre, I managed to free myself from the terrible slavery of drugs. I couldn't believe it. I had thrown eight years of life away through that damn heroin and now, finally free, I could get back to living again. After a few months however, I started to feel unwell, to have a temperature, headaches and other strange symptoms. It was terrible to discover that from the result of the blood tests that I had full-blown AIDS. Do you see why I am condemned to death? For a month now I've been living in a parish centre. Knowing my condition they let me sleep there. The other young people sleeping there all have AIDS too, and to see them dying right there in front of me day after day only increases my anguish. This is why, when I don't feel too bad, I prefer to spend my time out

56

on the streets, where I had lived for years anyway, and beg a bit of money so that I can do something to make me feel a bit better."

"Don't you have a family, anyone you could stay with?"

"A family? You're joking! I've never had one. My mother abandoned us when we were little (I've got a younger brother who is still on drugs), my father's an alcoholic, so we got quite a few beatings. Now he is living like a tramp somewhere, I don't know where. And as for friends, when you live for years focussed on your next 'fix', nothing else exists. You meet up with others only to use them for the only thing that matters to you, which is your next dose of heroin. Inevitably you lose your old friends and you're not able to make any new ones."

"And at the centre where you are staying, have you not made any friends there?"

"There are three or four really good lads there who come in as volunteers, but they are very busy. You know what it's like. No one likes to look death in the face." I knew very well what he meant, because I had been to visit a house for AIDS victims in Rome several times. The young volunteers came two or three times, but they couldn't handle it and so they didn't come again. So, apart from the nuns who worked there, and they were working hard as nurses, there weren't many other visitors and the residents, not having anyone to relate to, had to live their most difficult moments alone.

"I was really ill for a number of years," I replied, "At a certain point the doctors told me I was suffering from chronic uveitis which eventually would probably have made me blind. They also suspected that I had Bechet's Syndrome, a very serious, incurable illness."

"So, you know very well what I mean; you will surely have felt the same desperation and the same fear that sometimes grips me."

I honestly didn't know how to explain to him that, thanks to God, despite my terrible sufferings and the worrying prognosis, I had never despaired, but had always kept a great inner peace. Nevertheless, I had understood perfectly how desperate I would have felt in his situation.

I tried to give some sort of answer.

"To be honest with you, I did get very close to despair. I was gradually losing my sight, my physical sufferings were atrocious and the possibility that I might become blind worried me more than the thought of death. However, I had a really beautiful experience, which was the greatest miracle for me. During the whole of this long period of illness, I experienced a very deep joy and I saw death not as a condemnation, but as a beautiful moment, as a release from physical suffering and as a chance to fly up into the heaven of love."

"Really? How was it possible that despite everything you were at peace. I too am a Christian and I believe in the possibility of life after death, but it doesn't mean that physical suffering and death don't scare me stiff!"

"This is normal, it's part of human nature, but in the Gospel it is written that what is impossible to man is possible to God and that 'the fruits of the Spirit are peace, joy, love…'"

"What do you mean? Explain it to me, it interests me a lot."

"I mean that humanly for me too it would have been impossible to live my illness serenely and not be very afraid of death. But if we try to live our suffering with love, for love, in love, God, who is love, can make the impossible possible and can transform fear into peace. But you need an intense prayer life and a strong intention to let yourself be guided by the Spirit, by conscience and not by the flesh, because peace is a fruit of the Spirit and a great grace from God. For me it was also possible thanks to the support of lots of people."

"How I would like to experience a bit of peace," he commented, "instead of this anguish! To tell you the truth in certain moments I have managed it, but sometimes it just seems impossible."

"It isn't impossible, I assure you! Think about St Francis who still fascinates half the world. He is remembered as the saint of joy, and yet think of the terrible sufferings he had to endure. Just the stigmata itself must have been a martyrdom: wounds that pierce the hands and feet and the rib cage – not to mention the hunger and the cold, the blindness and all the other illnesses he suffered!"

"I see what you mean... With all that he went through... how did he manage to experience joy? Well, he must have been a saint!"

"But he wasn't born a saint! He was a poor sinner like me and you. He became a saint, probably because he knew how to give value to suffering and to live it with Christ, through Christ and in Christ."

"Yes, but my faith is still too small. Until quite recently I didn't even believe, and I don't know Christ very well!"

"If you seek Him with all your heart, He will reveal

Himself more and more and he will carry all your crosses with you, making them lighter."

"How can I seek Him?"

"Begin by reading the Gospel and trying to live it. There you will discover an inestimable treasure and you will get to know something of the love of the one who created us and loved us to the point of letting himself be crucified so that neither you nor I would be alone on our cross."

"I would like to talk to you more about this. I felt very discouraged, but now a strand of hope has been reignited in me. But I have to go. I didn't realise how late it is and they are very keen on punctuality in the centre where I am staying. But I very much hope you will come and visit me at the centre some evening. I'll leave you my address or, if you want, you can often find me here in the daytime!"

He hurriedly wrote down his address on the back of a bus ticket and gave it to me saying, "Be careful. Don't lose it. I really do want to see you again!"

"Yes, I'll come and see you! I promise."

"Great!"

He shook my hand and set off at a brisk pace, but he stopped abruptly and said: "Hey, there's something important you didn't tell me! How is your health now? It seems your sight is OK and you look in good form!"

"Yes, you're right. I'm fine and my sight is now perfect."

"How come? Didn't you say they had diagnosed you with a chronic, incurable illness?"

"I'll tell you next time about how I received this immense gift. Anyway, I told you: nothing's impossible to God!"

"It's incredible... Hey, you've not even told me your name."

"You're right. My Name is Chiara. And yours?"

"My name's David."

"Bye David, see you later!"

"See you later. I'm counting on you, eh!"

I continued walking down the street when a nice young man with a rucksack, a penny whistle and a dog came up to me. I stopped to look at him, intrigued by the jaunty tune he was playing. He stopped playing and said:

"Music is beautiful. It's one way of staying cheerful! And then playing in the street you can always make a bit of money to buy something to eat."

John was a very sociable young man and very chatty and he too told me many things about his life including how he came to live on the streets. He had suffered a lot and had been subjected to a lot of violence. He had had all sorts of experiences but without ever feeling really satisfied; once he had even attempted suicide, but they had managed to save him...

I had imagined that the world of the street would be full of people weighed down with suffering, and when I actually came face to face with these sufferings the impact was very strong.

In just one day I had seen despair, violence, darkness and anguish of every sort and I felt the sufferings of all those I had met within me. But I had also seen smiles of hope and consolation flowering. Once again I had experienced His wonders. A bit of listening and a bit of love were enough for "Something" very beautiful to colour each meeting. At the end of our long chat, John was able to say:

"I didn't believe in God, but now I think I was wrong. God is here; I feel His presence right now."

"I was really amazed by his intuition: God was really present in our midst and even John, who didn't believe in Him, realised it!"

Once again I had experienced the mystery contained in the Word of God, which assures us that whatever we do to one of the "least", we do to Him. In fact, I hadn't met "drug addicts", "vagabonds" or "alcoholics" – I had met Jesus crucified alive! I had met brothers of mine who were in some kind of death, but I felt myself loving them as brothers.

New Horizons

For a long time I had been feeling a strong call to consecrate myself completely to God, but it wasn't easy to discern the kind of consecration to which he was calling me. It was clear that it wasn't to enclose myself within the walls of a convent, but rather to live completely immersed in the world, giving my "sin" to God so that He, the Omnipotent, could make of it an instrument of love for those who had never known love, of peace for those who lived in anguish, of life for those who lived in "death": *"The wages of sin is death"* (Rm 6: 23).

I was feeling an increasingly pressing desire to say, with St Paul: *"I know only Christ and him crucified"* and I wanted to spend my life looking for and loving Him, a living crucifix, in many of my brothers and sisters. I knew that it was important to find the right "connection" in the Church by taking vows (*"I am the vine and you are the branches, without me you can do nothing"*), because you can't immerse yourself in "hell" if you're not closely connected to the vine... it wasn't easy! All the men and women of God I asked were quite convinced of the vocation I felt, but they told me that, as regards the vow of obedience, I would have to make it, either in a community that was already living the same vocation as mine, or directly to the bishop. I tried for a long time to find someone who was already living the same call as me, but they didn't seem to exist. There were plenty of communities of consecrated persons that were dedicated to the poor, the sick and the suffering, but I couldn't find any that had chosen the hell of the streets as their mission field. So I decided to ask the Heavenly Mother, issuing one of my usual *ultimata*: "Listen Mother," I said, "if possible, help me meet someone this week who lives in deep communion with God and who will confirm that this call I feel to consecrate myself completely to God with special care for my brothers and sisters with problems of drug addiction, alcoholism, prostitution, AIDS and prison comes from God, and that they will help me understand to whom I should make my vow of Obedience." I also thought that it would be nice if this person were my own bishop because, some time ago, during a mass I had attended by chance, he had said something about the mystery of the cross which was very important for me. Two days later, my joy and my surprise were uncontainable when I went to recollect myself in prayer for a moment in the university chapel only to find that the bishop was celebrating mass there. As soon as I set foot in the chapel, Bishop Boccaccio was saying: "Because you see, sometimes Jesus passes and knocks on the door of our hearts calling us to follow him in a radical way. And perhaps he is asking us: will you love me in this brother or sister who has AIDS, who takes drugs, who is a prostitute who lives on the streets or who is in prison? It is He who is calling us and we shouldn't be afraid to give Him our yes, in saying our 'Here I am'."

The promptness and the precision of the reply that I was awaiting were once again mind-blowing. In my five years at university I had never bumped into the bishop in the chapel and now, not only was I meeting him, but it seemed as if the words he was uttering when I walked into the chapel had been put into his mouth by Our Lady specially for me. So, after mass I went to the bishop to confide my problem to him about how to discern my vocation – it was a decisive moment of God. I had found, finally, the connection to the "Vine" which had been thought out by God's love for me.

When the day of my consecration arrived I experienced an incredible joy. The vows were nothing other than the cutting off of the chains, of the attachment to things, persons and projects which often bind us and stop us from flying in the heaven of God's love. I really felt as if I was flying and I was in contemplation of the ineffable mystery contained in the word of God: "I will make you my spouse forever."

I thought: "You, the King of kings, the Eternal, the Immense, the Omnipotent, not only did you become man and give your life for me, not only do you make yourself bread in the Eucharistic mystery so that I can feed myself with you, but you even make yourself my spouse? It's too much, it's too great, it's too beautiful!"

Then I went straight to Termini station because I wanted to celebrate the occasion with my friends there. Straightaway I bumped into Michela who embraced me very warmly. She was covered in mud because it was raining and she had just fallen. With tears in her eyes she told me many things, above all that she was on the streets again because her mother had kicked her out. So she couldn't do the course of treatment in the community she had wanted to do. In fact, that programme requires several months of preparation before the person can enter the community, during which they have to be accompanied by a relative and have a house to sleep in. She said to me, weeping: "Please Chiara take me away from here, take me home with you. I don't want to go back to prostitution and drug-taking!" I saw in her that living crucifix to which I had just consecrated my life and it was such a suffering not to be able to take Michela home with me, that I saw very clearly how important it was to find a house where I could welcome all my friends.

I had been going to the station for two years and too often I had felt the same intense suffering. Until then it seemed clear to me that all I had to do was go there, share, point people in the direction of the appropriate place (I had a map with all the social centres, hostels and soup kitchens in the area) and then disappear again to avoid people becoming dependent on me. Nevertheless, I had noticed that, despite the fact that we were in the capital, the social structures were completely inadequate and insufficient.

There were so many young people whom I didn't know where to send and I suffered a great deal because I knew that most of those who landed at Termini, having lived through really very difficult situations, immediately found plenty of people of the organised underworld ready to entice them with alluring proposals for making a quick buck; it was very difficult for them to come across a brother or sister ready to reach out and together help them get through the difficult moments.

At Termini there was a nightly volunteer service; there were even shifts organised by various associations and parish groups, but they concentrated mainly on "tramps", to whom they distributed sandwiches, hot drinks and blankets, as well as a little human warmth. It was difficult however, for anyone to set foot in the "hotter" areas where there were drugs, prostitution and the underworld; and yet there was a desperate need there for a bit of love and solidarity. More than one young person had confessed to me that they had wept with joy after meeting me, because in ten or fifteen years of life on the streets they had never come across anyone who had stopped and shown an interest in them without an ulterior motive. The sentence that Angelo and some of his friends had written on a wall: "Despite your indifference, we exist," left a powerful impression on me, and, in fact, I came across this wall of indifference every evening. How often I had helped young people who had collapsed and had been lying for ages on the ground, freezing, in front of crowds of people at Termini, who simply quickened their pace so as not to get involved and not to feel reproached by their consciences! How often I have taken on the despair of young people who felt incapable of freeing themselves from the tentacles of the vicious circles into which they had fallen; they had arrived perhaps from Eastern Europe, in pursuit of the mirage of an honest job to help get out of the miserable conditions in which they were living, only to find themselves enslaved and totally exploited by "protectors", without even having the chance of making a phone call. I had met others who had been released from prison, fully intending to mend their ways but totally discouraged because of the difficulty of finding work with a criminal record and no fixed abode, when of course you can't rent accommodation if you don't have a job. Then there were others who had to take up prostitution to pay for drugs and those who took up drugs to have the courage to work as prostitutes. I've met young people with slashes and scars and broken teeth, the results of trying to escape from the grip of the "protectors".

How sad it is when we realise how quick we are to judge and to condemn, but how great Jesus' words are: *"Whoever is without sin, let him cast the first stone."* How much suffering could be avoided if, instead of casting stones, we could bend down and get up with whoever, like us, has fallen. Already, lots of young people had asked me to take them away from there and I could only stay there and suffer with them, feeling a desolate sense of impotence. I thought often about all my new friends and especially about Cristina. She was only 18 and had run away from home because her brothers and father were raping her. She had just started taking drugs and had discovered that the boy she had fallen in love with was a "protector" whose sole aim was to put her on the streets. She too had already started working as a prostitute. She had embraced me with tears in her eyes, saying: "Please Chiara, take me away from this hell, take me home with you or to any other place; I don't want to live like this." But I myself was a guest in a house belonging to three other girls and couldn't allow myself the luxury of bringing anyone home to stay. All I could do was give her the addresses of a few communities, but I knew how difficult it was to get through all the red tape and how difficult, if not impossible, to get a place for people in situations like Cristina's.

So, I started to talk to some of my friends about my "crazy" idea of a house to welcome these young people. We started to meet and to pray together to understand what we needed to do. Already in September, Loredana had told me that she felt a strong call to live a consecrated life like me. In January, a bit jokingly and a bit seriously, we started talking to Lucia who had told us of her desire to open a family house and to set up projects.

I liked the idea of a family house, because I was very keen that the people who came to live there should be able to live in an atmosphere of warmth and affection. But I was thinking more along the lines of the early Christians where we would be able to live together having the Gospel as the only rule of our life. In the desire to live the Gospel as far as possible to the letter and to open ourselves up to welcome everybody, especially my friends from the station, our intention was to create a "bridge" between the street and the existing social structures.

In January, that all seemed a long way off, but I proposed to Lucia that we should give a name to the community: "What would you think," I said to her, "if we were to call it 'New Horizons'! The horizon is the meeting point between heaven and earth and I would like everyone who comes into our community, committing themselves to live the word of God, to experience something of Heaven here on this earth. I would like to see the miracle of *'Where two or three are united in my name, I am in their midst'* (Mt 18: 20), that the hell lived by whoever is welcomed here to be transformed into Paradise. And then the Word of God will let us see 'those things that the eye cannot see, the ear cannot hear, that will never enter into man's heart' and will open up ever new horizons, Jesus is the one who makes all things new."

Lucia was not against the name "New Horizons" and the other girls to whom I mentioned it were also quite in

favour of it. They also liked the idea of the proposed programme. We knew that we were launching a fairly bold
project, but we wanted to do things as well as possible.

We drew up a programme which immediately gained
the support of the St Vincent de Paul Society, Caritas and
the trade unions, and at that time it seemed that the City
Council in Rome were happy to give us both funding and a
building. But, after several months of continuous wrangling
with the "black hole" of Roman bureaucracy, we still hadn't
managed to get anything. So I decided that, having tried
to follow the advice of the wise and the prudent, the time
had arrived to change track. We put all our hope into an
infallible bank, the bank of Providence – there aren't any
other banks that offer interest at one hundred to one! The
Gospel speaks clearly: it promises the hundredfold to
whoever leaves everything for the kingdom of God.

Seek the Kingdom of God

"Therefore I tell you, do not worry about your life, what you will eat or drink; or about your body, what you will wear [...] Look at the birds of the air; they do not sow or reap or store away in barns, and yet your heavenly Father feeds them. Are you not much more valuable than they? [...]See how the lilies of the field grow. They do not labour or spin. Yet I tell you that not even Solomon in all his splendour was dressed like one of these [...] But seek first his kingdom and his righteousness, and all these things will be given to you as well"(Mt 6: 25-26, 28-29, 33).

"Sell everything you have and give to the poor, and you will have treasure in heaven. Then come, follow me" (Lk 18: 22).

It wasn't the first time I had meditated on these marvellous words, but that day on the Polbrodo, the hill of the apparitions at Medjugorje, I felt they were being addressed to me personally with a completely new strength and I felt the deepest desire to live them as literally as possible.

"Look at the birds of the air, the lilies of the field!"; "Go, sell everything! Good gracious, I hadn't sold everything! Certainly, I had been trying to live poverty for some time, but I had my little securities; I had a job, clothes, books...

"OK," I thought, "until the Eternal Father procures a house for us to welcome my brothers and sisters of the streets, I could go and live with them, I could try to live this life to the letter: leave my job, give everything to the poor and live like the lilies of the fields, keeping just a pair of jeans, a T-shirt and a Bible."

I liked the idea a lot, too much, to the point that the rational part of me started to get seriously worried and to prepare a counter-attack: "Come on Chiara, use a bit of common sense! This time you're really losing it! You're surely not thinking about camping in the open air? Have you already forgotten about how ill you were not so long ago? If you start to live on the streets and go to eat in the Caritas canteen, before long you will be ill again! And then… you're a girl, it's far too dangerous."

It was all true, but I had experienced many times just how much human and divine logic contrast with one another: the Word of God is truth and inasmuch as we try to live it to the letter, we allow our Heavenly Father to take the reins of our life in hand. Then, His own love can finally look after all our needs, great and small. I felt a very deep joy and incredible sense of freedom when my spiritual director assented to my desire to try this new experience. We fixed a date for leaving the house, the job and every other thing, to live with my brothers and sisters of the streets: 24 May, the Feast of Mary Help of Christians.

I had also confided my decision to Fr Ettore, a really great priest who often went to the station at night and who had brought several tramps to his parish to sleep. Fr Ettore, happy with my choice, said I could sleep in the school run by the sisters of the parish; in this way I could at least live to some extent the virtue of prudence.

The great day was approaching and even though I felt a bit afraid from time to time, joy was growing within me. Anyway, a week before the agreed starting date, my spiritual director told me that what was important was to take this step spiritually, but now, out of love for my parents and especially my father, whose weak heart might not hold out, it was better to continue looking for the house and to stop work only when I went to live there. Strangely, I wasn't very happy with this, but what was important to me was to do the will of God, and obedience is always a guarantee of that.

However, the love of God had prepared a great surprise for me: exactly on 24 May I received a phone call during which we were offered l'Isola (the Island), an attractive building with about 50 beds, four small apartments and three hectares of land with sheds. We could move in in December. On the same day, Fr Ettore rang to tell us that the Blessed Sacrament Sisters were offering us two large classrooms and a toilet, right next to the station, where Loredana, Sonia and Lucia and I could start our community life until we transferred to l'Isola. And finally, a third phone call on 24 May said we could open a day centre at the station, because we had been offered a place at Termini, right where we wanted it.

It was an incredible hundredfold! I had offered, only spiritually, a little room, three metres by three, where I slept, my clothes, my little securities and in response, exactly on the feast of Mary Help of Christians, we were offered, free of charge, places and buildings which were worth millions. What joy to contemplate the amazing imagination of the love of the Omnipotent Father.

To begin with it was difficult to believe that we would be able to cover our monthly outgoings which would be around 18 thousand euros, given that all our wages together came to just about 3 thousand euros. Loredana, Giacomo and I had left our jobs to work for the community and Tonino had a part-time job. But it was wonderful to experience that for every need we could leap trustfully into the arms of Providence, and we never lacked anything.

The timeliness and the precision of His intervention are really very moving, as can be seen even in the little things. You hardly have time even to express a wish than it is immediately fulfilled. I have seen an infinite number of instances of this. I'd like to recount a few little examples, so that everyone can participate in the amazement and the joy with which we experience the attentive love of our Heavenly Father.

One morning I awoke with the thought of a bill for 583 euros fixed in my head. We only had 180 euros, which we needed to buy basic food supplies. For a few moments I thought to myself: "Are you sure you're trying to live the Gospel to the letter, or are you not just a naïve person who is dragging others along with you in an absurd project? All the other communities are well organised, they pay the young people, they receive subsidies, fixed payments on which they can depend. In a nutshell, they can guarantee a certain security to the people they take in. Most of the religious institutes, who certainly live the Gospel, have their own economy, their balance sheets, their secure sources of economic support. And you, with this faith in Providence, for how long do you think you can carry on feeding twenty hungry mouths, pay the bills, the medical expenses, transport costs etc?"

These thoughts had crept into my soul causing some disturbance, but immediately faith in the word of God gave me back my peace: "Don't worry about what you will eat or drink... Seek the kingdom of God and Its justice and the rest will be given you as well." So, with a great sense of peace, I turned to Jesus and said: "Listen Jesus, perhaps I really am a bit naïve, I don't know... but the fact is that I've embarked on this crazy project simply because I love You and want, with all my strength and all my limitations, to seek Your kingdom and Your justice. So, I am sure that this time the rest will arrive as well. I won't wait with an anxious soul, I will concern myself only with seeking Your kingdom... and You will most certainly look after the bills!"

That afternoon, someone who wanted to know more about our community came to visit us. Before going he asked if he could leave a small contribution and he pressed a sealed envelope into my hand. As soon as I had a spare moment I went into my room, opened the envelope and carefully counted the money so as to write down the amount in our book of Providence. I counted the money, and then counted it again: incredible! There was exactly 583 euros!

Another morning the young people were all working in the different sectors of the community and I went into the kitchen to see how things were going. Paolo who was working there that day said: "Chiara, I'm sorry, but I won't be able to cook much of a lunch today, we've only got a bit of pasta. There's nothing for the main course."

"Don't worry; a nice plate of pasta is always welcome. And anyway a bit of fasting now and then doesn't do any harm!"

The words had hardly left my mouth when the intercom phone rang. It was a lad I didn't know. He said his job was transporting frozen foods. A doctor friend of his had told him about the community and had asked him to bring us some frozen food. He had brought us God's providence, and we had an exquisite main course not only on that day, but for the rest of the week.

Every time you take someone in from the street there is always a competition amongst the others to clothe them, as when they arrive they are almost always shabbily dressed. So, someone will offer their jumper, another a shirt or a pair of trousers, and in a very short time the new arrival will have their wardrobe renewed. One day a young man arrived who had only the shirt, trousers and shoes he stood up in; he was quite a big lad too. There was only one other lad in the house the same size, and he had very little himself. The following morning a lady arrived with a large bag of clothes. You can imagine my joy when I saw what was in the bag: trousers, jumpers, shirts, jackets, underwear, scarves... and the size was exactly that of the lad who had just arrived!

What never fails to surprise me is the fact that Providence is so timely and not only with regard to basic needs, but also for simple little wishes. One day, for example, Francesca, a girl who had had a very hard time on the streets with drugs and prison, told us that for a long time she had had a secret desire: to have a fluffy toy! This was something quite important for her, for to survive on the street she had always had to appear strong and hard. So, Loredana thought it would be nice to give her such a gift when possible. But, as always, the love of the Father wanted to beat us to it. That same afternoon someone knocked on the door with a selection of gifts. And, of course, among all these gifts, there was a fluffy toy, which filled Francesca with happiness.

Another big problem in community are teeth. Almost all young people who have taken drugs have terrible teeth. I put off addressing this problem for as long as possible, because knowing dentists' fees, the cost of treating just one person would have been astronomical. But when Annamaria started getting terrible toothache I decided to take her to Carlo, a very good dentist and family friend. I asked for an estimate, just to have an idea of the cost. You can imagine my surprise when he insisted that he didn't want anything, not even for the expensive materials he was using. He told me he would also be very happy to treat all the young people of the community free of charge. In two years I don't know how many young people he treated, but if we had had to pay it would have made us bankrupt.

I could recount hundreds of fascinating stories like these, but we would need an entire book just for them. To begin with we had three small salaries, but now we don't even have these, because we have all left our jobs to dedicate ourselves full-time to the community. Our only fixed incomes are a monthly contribution from the St Vincent de Paul Society which helps us pay the rent, and a thousand Euros or so which we earn from our art and craft workshop. Everything else, and that comes to a considerable amount, is completely entrusted to the imagination of Providence. So, the subtleties of God's love, both great and small, which we experience every day, are infinite, thanks to the generosity of many, many people who, from time to time, have wanted to become instruments of Providence for us. It is amazing to be able to contemplate the beauty of "all these things will be given to you as well" which the Father never fails to give to his children.

Aspire to the Gifts

The date fixed for our move to l'Isola, the beautiful building which had been offered to us, was 28 December. First of all we wanted to do a nine-day retreat to deepen together our understanding of the passages of Scripture regarding the Holy Spirit. We wanted to finish our retreat by asking the gift of the Holy Spirit for each one of us on the feast of the Baptism of Jesus.

We were well aware of the fact that we weren't prepared humanly for the project we were about to undertake. To take in people from the streets with problems of drug addiction, alcoholism, AIDS, prostitution and prison... is a huge commitment! But we also knew that *"What is impossible for man is possible for God"* (Lk 18: 27), and we wanted to prepare ourselves to be docile instruments of the action of the Holy Spirit and to allow Him to guide our every step. We had also understood that *"our struggle is not against flesh and blood, but against the rulers, against the authorities, against the powers of this dark world and against the spiritual forces of evil in the heavenly realms"* (Eph 6: 12). So we had to *"Put on the full armour of God so that you can take your stand against the devil's schemes"* (Eph 6: 11), acquire the necessary arms, trying not to be ignorant in our knowledge of the gifts of the Spirit: *"Now about spiritual gifts, brothers, I do not want you to be ignorant"* (1 Cor 12: 1).

Already, before moving to the new premises there had been no lack of opportunity to do some "training" in this sense. The first such opportunity was once again my health. For three months I had had a series of symptoms which, taking into consideration what had happened before, had given the doctors serious cause for concern, so much so that in October, after the results of the latest blood tests which weren't very encouraging, the doctor wanted me back in hospital. I asked if it could wait for nine days, saying that if the tests were still negative after that I would go into hospital.

We were meditating at that time on living the Word of God to the letter, and one of the Words that was coming back to me time and again was: "And these will be the signs that will accompany those who believe... they lay hands on the sick and they will be healed."

It is written: "Those who believe in me!" not those who are holy or who have special gifts. So, we're talking about a confirmation of our faith in Jesus.

So, I decided to ask Loredana and Sonia to pray for me with the laying on of hands. It was a great trial of faith for all of us: we had to overcome self-love, human respect and logical reasoning. The fact is that with the simplicity of children Loredana and Sonia started to pray for my healing, laying their hands on me. Our heavenly Father was very happy to give us this gift, perhaps also to show us the importance of living to the letter what his Word suggests to us. There was no need for me to go into hospital, because all the symptoms had disappeared and the results of the blood tests were normal.

For the four days before our move to l'Isola it was as if we had been hit by a hurricane. One after the other, those of us who had decided to go and live there were struck by strange, sudden and mysterious symptoms: one with a very high temperature accompanied by intolerable suffering, one by a heart attack, one tortured by agonising spasms and, to cap it all, Simona was diagnosed with uveitis. I couldn't believe it: the very illness that had provoked my extremely hard Calvary... and such a rare illness too! We prayed for each one with the laying on of hands, with faith in the power contained in the Word of God lived to the letter, and the fruits were immediate and surprising for all of us.

The 28 December, the long awaited date of our move, finally arrived. It was marked with plenty of difficulties and was also the beginning of our retreat. The building was ideal and we were delighted at last to have the possibility of welcoming our brothers and sisters in difficulty and despair. The last day of the retreat was an incredible celebration for all of us, which left an indelible mark on our hearts. It felt as if we were reliving, in a small way, the wonders of Pentecost and we were moved and amazed by the presence of the love of God. There were about thirty of us; many still had problems with drink or drugs. It was already nine in the evening and we just couldn't leave the chapel, despite the fact that we had prayed all day, apart from a break for lunch. We really did feel "inebriated" with the Holy Spirit and our wonder was immense as we contemplated the marvellous things He was doing for each one of us. Many of us found ourselves "singing in tongues"[3] and although we couldn't understand what was happening, we were contemplating

[3] Many passages of Scripture refer to the gift of tongues: Mk 16:17; Acts 2: 4 & 10, 45-46; Rm 8: 26; 1 Cor 12, 10 & 14ff.

with the simplicity of children the power and the beauty of prayer that the Holy Spirit was giving us. The "singing in tongues" was accompanied by tears of joy, of freedom and of conversion, of healing and by touching words of prophecy that were specific and prompt. Some, under the powerful action of the Holy Spirit, fell into the "sleep of the Spirit" – an intense spiritual experience during which consciousness, though still vigilant, has a moment of abandonment similar to sleep – and you wake with the feeling of having tasted something of the joy of Paradise. It soon became clear that the Eternal Father planned his own therapy for the young people that we would gather and he wanted, first of all, to show us the instruments needed. Later on, in fact, it was thanks to these many strong moments of prayer that Jesus spoke to, healed, freed and transformed the young people who came to the community deeply marked by experiences with drugs, prostitution or adherence to satanic sects.

At the end of the retreat we left full of enthusiasm and set out a programme which was as functional as possible to help the people we had welcomed, a programme which we still use today. Our daily timetable is as follows:

7.00-8.00: wake up, breakfast and room tidying

8.00-8.30: meditation together – a sentence from the Gospel is chosen to live out during the day.

8.40-13.00: work. We divided the work into different sectors: an art and craft workshop to make pottery, icons, lamp shades and various small items; the production of a musical which tells the story of the search for something to give meaning to our lives, and the joy of having found it; the cultivation of a small orchard; the kitchen and cleaning.

13.00-14.00: lunch.

14.00-14.45: silence (time dedicated to reading, relaxing, personal reflection, prayer).

14.45-15.30: adoration (optional).

15.30-18.30: work.

18.30-20.00: groups and sport. There are various groups, but all have the aim of helping personal development. There is the *sharing* group, in which they face up to what they are living, the difficulties encountered, any steps ahead taken, the joy of any discoveries, all read in the light of the Word of God meditated upon; then there is the *truth* group, in which, time by time, lots are drawn and all the other members of the group say what is positive or what can be improved, about the one drawn out of the hat; the *technical meeting* group asks for suggestions and ideas as to how to improve life in community; the *self-awareness* group, whose aim is to reveal all the negative attitudes, source of unhappiness for us and for others, which all of us, more or less consciously, tend to assume; it's a question of trying to identify the trap that generates them, the destructive effects, and the instruments required to modify such attitudes. And finally, there is the *spiritual formation* group in which we try to deepen our understanding of certain aspects of spirituality particularly useful for achieving inner peace.

20.00-21.00: supper.

21.15-22.00: creativity, meeting of the leaders and, once a week, an hour of adoration and praise – a very intense moment of spontaneous community prayer, open to all our friends who don't live in community. The main aim of this meeting is thanksgiving. Normally we focus our attention on what is lacking, but to thank God for all that he has freely given us is very helpful, not only spiritually, because it helps deepen our prayer, but also at a psychological level.

22.15: we end the day with a moment of community prayer and an examination of conscience, where we look back over the points of the house "rules".

We ask everyone to respect the timetable and the following house rules:

1) *"In everything, do to others what you would have them do to you"* (Mt 7: 12).

2) *"Be merciful, just as your Father is merciful. Do not judge, and you will not be judged. Do not condemn, and you will not be condemned. Forgive, and you will be forgiven. Give, and it will be given to you. A good measure, pressed down, shaken together and running over, will be poured into your lap. For with the measure you use, it will be measured to you"* (Lk 36-38).

3) *"If someone is caught in a sin, you who are spiritual should restore him gently. But watch yourself, or you also may be tempted. Carry each other's burdens"* (Gal 6: 1-2).

4) *"Live by the Spirit, and you will not gratify the desires of the sinful nature. For the sinful nature desires what is contrary to the Spirit, and the Spirit what is contrary to the sinful nature. They are in conflict with each other, so that you do not do what you want' [...] The acts of the sinful nature are obvious: sexual immorality, impurity and debauchery; idolatry and witchcraft; hatred, discord, jealousy, fits of rage, selfish ambition, dissensions, factions and envy;*

drunkenness, orgies, and the like. I warn you, as I did before, that those who live like this will not inherit the kingdom of God. But the fruit of the Spirit is love, joy, peace, patience, kindness, goodness, faithfulness, gentleness and self-control" (Gal 5: 16-17 & 19ff).

5) *"Therefore each of you must put off falsehood and speak truthfully to his neighbour, for we are all members of one body. In your anger do not sin: Do not let the sun go down while you are still angry, and do not give the devil a foothold [...]Do not let any unwholesome talk come out of your mouths, but only what is helpful for building others up according to their needs, that it may benefit those who listen. And do not grieve the Holy Spirit of God, with whom you were sealed for the day of redemption* (Eph 4: 25-27 & 29ff).

6) *"Let us love one another, for love comes from God. Everyone who loves has been born of God and knows God [...] since God so loved us, we also ought to love one another. No-one has ever seen God; but if we love one another, God lives in us and his love is made complete in us"* (1 Jn 4: 7 & 11ff).

7) *"As the Father has loved me, so have I loved you. Now remain in my love. If you obey my commands, you will remain in my love, just as I have obeyed my Father's commands and remain in his love. I have told you this so that my joy may be in you and that your joy may be complete. My command is this: Love each other as I have loved you. Greater love has no-one than this, that he lay down his life for his friends"* (Jn 15: 9-13).

8) *"Love the Lord your God with all your heart and with all your soul and with all your mind and with all your*

strength. *The second [commandment] is this: 'Love your neighbour as yourself.' There is no commandment greater than these"* (Mk 12 30-31).

9) *"In this you greatly rejoice, though now for a little while you may have had to suffer grief in all kinds of trials. These have come so that your faith— of greater worth than gold, which perishes even though refined by fire— may be proved genuine and may result in praise, glory and honour when Jesus Christ is revealed"* (1 Pt I: 6-7).

10) *"Be joyful always; pray continually; give thanks in all circumstances, for this is God's will for you in Christ Jesus"* (1 Thess 5:16-18). Tend towards perfection, take courage with one another, have the same sentiments, live in the peace of the love of God and peace will always be with you.

11) *"I urge you to live a life worthy of the calling you have received. Be completely humble and gentle; be patient, bearing with one another in love. Make every effort to keep the unity of the Spirit through the bond of peace. There is one body and one Spirit"* (Eph 4: 1-4).

12) *"So do not worry, saying, 'What shall we eat?' or 'What shall we drink?' or 'What shall we wear?' For the pagans run after all these things, and your heavenly Father knows that you need them. But seek first his kingdom and his righteousness, and all these things will be given to you as well"*(Mt 6: 31-33).

13) *"Do not conform to the evil desires you had when you lived in ignorance. But just as he who called you is holy, so be*

holy in all you do; for it is written: Be holy, because I am holy" (1 Pt 1: 14-16).

While knowing full well how difficult it is for anyone who has lived on the streets for many years to take on a commitment like this, we put our cards on the table straightaway, explaining that "to offer a fish" does not interest us so much as to "teach them how to fish". In other words, we don't want just to offer a hot meal and a warm bed, the things that might temporarily alleviate unhappiness, we want to get to the roots of it, following the way the Creator himself has shown us to reach the fullness of joy: *"I have told you this so that my joy may be in you and that your joy may be complete" (Jn 15: 11)* and have peace in their hearts: *"Peace I leave with you; my peace I give you. I do not give to you as the world gives"* (Jn14: 27).

Now I Feel Free

Help me, I can't make it

I started to use drugs when I was a young lad, a bit out of curiosity, a bit so as not to feel the odd one out with my friends on the streets. In my area almost all the young people were 'off their heads' in one way or another and if you didn't conform to a certain image, you felt out of it. I started by smoking a bit of hash and drinking, but then I wanted to try different things, things that were newer and stronger. This is how I came to be trapped into a cocaine habit for fifteen years, and how I started to sell drugs as well. In the beginning I thought I had found what I was looking for, I was blinded by the fact that I could have money in my pocket, a nice car and everything that seemed important to me. I was convinced that what was important was to buy everything and everybody.

The more I had the more I wanted, the more 'off my head' I was the more I wanted to be so... I always wanted more and so some serious problems started to come out. Heroin is a substance that takes away your will to live. Many die with a syringe in their arm and I could have easily been one of them. You lose everything because of drugs. You do anything so you can have your fix, betray anyone. So I began to go in and out of prison. When I was in prison I would reflect a bit and come to realise that I had lost absolutely everything, that I had abandoned my family, learnt not to look anyone in the face... and to be completely alone! But then when I came out of prison I would take up the old life again, unable to free myself from heroin. I asked myself where all this was leading, what I had achieved, where all my friends, with whom I had lived better times, had gone... the dreams? One day, when I really was desperate, I raised my eyes to heaven and, with the syringe in my arm, I cried out: "God, if you exist, help me. I've had enough. I can't carry on like this. If you're there, do something for me." A short time later I bumped into a friend who told me about Chiara and her community, where they try to live the Gospel. I had made an attempt before with a community, but then I carried on taking drugs. I was afraid that I wouldn't be able to leave my past behind me and to start again from scratch. As soon as I arrived at New Horizons I felt welcomed and I felt a new peace. I had the impression that God himself was taking me by the hand and was asking me to start again with Him.

Chiara was a simple 28 year-old girl who had chosen to live amidst young people, criminals of every sort, without worrying about the possible dangers. I thought she must have been mad to have made a choice like that, but I was immediately struck by her and decided to stay in the community.

To begin with I had a certain difficulty in trying to live the Gospel and enter into prayer because my previous life had been just the opposite... sex, drugs, money and rock and roll. However, gradually, doing the meditation that we do every day in community, I had the impression that a certain kind of "spiritual cleansing" was happening within me. Someone was purifying all my negativity. The words of the Gospel were hurting me, but they were healing my heart... like a surgical operation. I experienced that where there is charity life is reborn. I was welcomed into the community with great love and patience, and I was accepted for who I was. I was given everything, food, clothing, they taught me how to work, to pray... things I didn't know. I discovered that at the basis of everything is the love of God and that, as St Augustine says, God created our heart for him and we find peace only when we return to Him.

And it's thanks to this free gift of love that you receive in community, that many young people who arrive torn apart by wounds, turn to God and rediscover the joy of living.

When I arrived at New Horizons I had spiritual, moral and psychological problems... now with the Lord's help and that of the people he has put beside me, I have been able to overcome these problems.

Now I feel free from the weight of the drugs, I feel that the Lord is carrying it with me. I am no longer afraid of falling back into that world, as I did when I came out of prison, because I have acquired a security that I didn't know before. I have understood that the only thing that counts is to love, to be ready to give our lives for one another; to persevere right to the end, free from our selfishness, our passions, our judgements and prejudices. In the end we will be asked how much we have loved, and this is all that remains. And even if at times the road seems a bit narrow, and we are consumed by suffering, love generates life for us and for others and takes us along a way of sanctity unrecognised by our eyes but clear to Jesus. Whoever loses his life for the Lord will find it and if we try to become like children we will be able to enter the Kingdom of Heaven.

I feel I can say that hell exists for everyone, but everyone is free to choose either to stay on his own or learn to walk towards paradise. God became man, he was crucified for us. So we too are called to help whoever, like us, has been or still is in darkness. And helping others you discover that the Lord carries your burden and that only in this way are you truly free.

Paolo

You saved me from darkness

I was born in a faraway land, into a large family of three girls and three boys.

We were quite well off and also a very united family until my father started to drink. His drinking got worse until he stopped work and stopped caring for us. Eventually he went off with another woman.

My mother started to sell her jewellery and her best clothes and did all sorts of jobs just to keep the wolf from the door.

She managed to earn quite a bit of money performing magic rites that she had learnt from her grandmother.

Despite this there was hardly anything to eat because there were so many mouths to feed. I had to leave school because we didn't have enough money and the situation continued to get worse. My father came home every three months and he was always drunk. He stole whatever money my mother had been able to earn and then disappeared again.

A 30 year-old man used to come and visit us frequently.

He always came with plenty of gold and money. He bought us clothes and gave us money.

One day he told me he had fallen in love with me and that he could find me a good job.

I was easily convinced and left home without saying anything to my mother.

When I arrived in Italy with him things changed immediately. He stole my documents and often beat me and forced me to become a prostitute, becoming my "protector".

I earned a lot of money but I had to give it all to him. Sometimes I had to go to Naples and to Turin to sell drugs. When we were travelling I would carry the drugs so that he was in no danger of being caught.

I started to smoke hash, to drink a lot and to sniff cocaine. I was frustrated and depressed. He refused to give me back my documents, even though he had taken a good 40 thousand euros as a result of my 'work'.

I just didn't know what to do, who to go to for help. I would have liked to try and go to the police about this man, but I was too scared. I knew that if I went to the police without any documents they would have sent me back home and either my protector would have caught me or would have killed one of my family.

In some way or other he would make me pay dearly. I was really desperate, but fortunately someone helped me to escape and brought me to the New Horizons community.

In the community I found young people who had had serious problems: drugs, AIDS, prison, young people without parents and without a home… and yet I saw them living together with love and in joy.

They had forgotten the past and were building a future. I decided to try it myself. I received a lot of love, tenderness and patience from those who welcomed me into the community and with the help of meditation, prayer and the spiritual way we follow together, my life has changed.

Since I discovered the Lord and his love for me, my problems have disappeared. It's not that I no longer feel the suffering of the past and the wounds it brought me, but the Lord has helped me to see the positive side of every situation.

The Lord knows what to do so that everything leads to good, even the most sorrowful of situations. It's just that my suffering was too big and I wasn't able to bear it on my own... but I soon realised that someone else was carrying my cross with me.

I've no longer felt alone. Gradually, as time passed and I watched the young people who had welcomed me into the community, I discovered that the inner joy that they had was definitely not coming from things around them but from God.

So I put all my efforts into learning how to love.

It was a beautiful challenge for me who was used to a completely different type of life, but I felt reborn.

The world and its illusions (sex, drugs, money) would never have filled that emptiness I felt in my heart. Since I met Jesus my life has really changed.

I have been living in community now for about two years. I have been baptised, made my first communion and been confirmed (I wasn't a Christian before).

I also want to consecrate my life to the Lord with promises of poverty, chastity and obedience.

Someone might think that my choice is a bit premature, but it's the least I can give to the Lord to thank him for having torn me away from darkness and given me his light.

Lidia

My life at the service of those who are in the dark

I'm 28 and I was a heroin addict for more than 10 years. I was born and grew up in the Trionfale area of Rome, an area full of problems: political struggle, violence, delinquency and drugs. Until I was 15 I was a sensitive soul, always ready to help my neighbour. I had all the qualifications necessary to become a professional footballer, but all of a sudden I was faced with loads of problems, both in my family and in my social life. I had lost my father when I was seven and, as the result of an illness, my mother was left paralyzed and in a wheelchair, unable even to speak, for more than 15 years. I had to learn quickly how to cope with suffering and pain. A series of difficulties led to the family being split up and as a reaction to this I completely isolated myself. I managed to share a bit just with my friends on the streets, we felt understood only by each other. When I was 10 we started to go to football together. We thought it was wonderful! Then, after the match we were on a high and we started getting into trouble. We also started to smoke reefers which soon made us go off our heads and we became violent. Most of my friends became addicted to heroin. For a year and a half I tried my very best to help them kick it, but they started to make fun of me because I wouldn't take it, so I too went into the heroin tunnel. From 1985, for more than 10 years, I couldn't stop and to come out of it became more and more difficult.

Heroin made me do things I never dreamt I would do: stealing and selling drugs. I was respected and feared by everyone. I lived in a hotel, had cars, money, people subject to my will. One Christmas Day, a few years ago, I suddenly realised that everything I had was not real, and in my conscience I felt I wanted genuine relationships, not false ones. Only then did I try to listen to myself, to take notice of my conscience. I didn't have time to take a practical decision, because two days later I was arrested for selling drugs. When I was released from prison the desire I felt to change my life was even stronger within me. So, I started going to the C.E.I.S, a community which offered a course lasting two and a half years. At the end of this period I realised that there were certain problems that hadn't been resolved. I threw myself into my work but after three months or so I was full of anxiety, stressed out and went into deep depression which took me back into the world of drugs. For three months I slept in cars near Termini station. I lived like this until I felt very strongly that this was not my way. The next morning I returned to the community I had been in before, but they could not take me because there was no one who could accompnay me. While I was walking away from there, a girl I had never set eyes on before gave me the phone number of New Horizons. I phoned them straightaway and after a few chats with them I entered the community. Nineteen months have now passed and I have found what I was really always looking for: a family. I rediscovered love, the joy of living, respect for others, trust, and above all, the real Michele. And all this thanks to a spiritual way.

It is now several months since I consecrated my life to the Lord with promises of poverty, chastity and obedience, and I've decided that from now on my life will be at the service of those who are in the dark, that same dark from which I emerged, thanks to the Lord.

I always had in my heart the dream of being able to help those young people who find themselves in the tunnel of drugs, and now that this dream is being fulfilled I feel a great joy. I am happy to return to my local area and to communicate to my old mates not the darkness of before, but the joy, the amazing value of life.

One of my friends followed me and now lives in community with us, and this is a wonderful thing the Lord has done for me. There's no shortage of work in community, But I can do it all with love for the other young people who come in off the streets, and instead of tiring me out, it fills me to the full.

For this and for everything I thank the Lord.

Michele (Michael)

Can we serve two masters?

Ever since I was small I had to struggle to survive. When I was one I was handed over to an institute and for three years or so I was subjected to every type of violence. After this terrible experience at last I was adopted. I thought the nightmare had come to an end, but less than a year later I was once more in a situation of continuous violence. My heart became harder and harder and it became impossible for me to believe in love and in respect for my neighbour. When I was 18 I decided to leave home and make my own life.

I became a chef and in just a few years reached a pretty high level of success. However, I became unscrupulous and ambitious and got into some bad company.

I had to work very long hours and to keep going at that rate I started to take cocaine, as well as drinking coffee, smoking and drinking. After 10 years my body started to feel the effects and I started to lose weight, get very nervous and was unable to sleep properly.

For me, money was my life. I was earning 8/9 thousand euros per month, but I wasn't satisfied. I always wanted more, but felt increasingly empty. One day, while on a journey, I read an article about Chiara and New Horizons. For me, the Gospel and Love were just a beautiful Utopia. I was living on another planet. What struck me though, was the fact that Chiara, a graduate in political science, had left everything to dedicate herself to the young people of the streets and to live with them. It seemed impossible to me and a kind of challenge grew within me. My heart told me I ought to talk to her as soon as possible and I managed eventually, despite umpteen difficulties, to meet her personally.

I arrived in the community at supper time and when Chiara saw me she came up to me and gave me a hug. In that moment I felt the embrace of a mother who is waiting for a child. That embrace was not a simple embrace between two people who meet, but it was that much higher embrace which takes place between the Father and the rediscovered son: the "prodigal son" who comes home. In that moment I discovered God and rediscovered Love. A woman had given "life" back to my dead soul. In that moment I understood that my life had to change radically and I asked myself: "Can I serve both God and money?" "No!"

In eleven days I decided to let everything go: career, house, friends... to go and live in community and to follow this marvellous adventure. It wasn't easy, especially the work, the worldly commitments and the 'environment' in which I lived; but now I can say that I have an immense joy in living, because I have discovered true freedom: God.

One of the most wonderful moments for me was when I consecrated my life to the Lord. Now I have nothing of my own, because we put everything in common, like the first Christian communities, but I feel really WEALTHY, because I have discovered the infinite love of God. Everything passes, only love remains.

Michela

The Dream

I had a marvellous dream that one day I would very much like to see realised. I dreamt of thousands of young people who, all at once, as if enchanted, shake themselves out of their heavy lethargy, which had made them vegetate for a long time, and who finally decide to live life to the full. Up until then they had all been feeding themselves on mortal food, consumerism, hedonism and individualism, and those who where not dead were sinking, agonisingly, in a long sleep.

They had lived for so many years in an unreal world, where every truth seems twisted, illusion looks like reality and reality illusion, the absurd seems logical and the logical absurd. They think they can grasp what turns out only to be smoke and they consider the things that don't pass away as impossible to grasp; the truth is considered a lie, a lie, truth; love is confused with selfishness and seen as madness.

One day the spirit of Love alighted on these young people and those who were dead came back to life, those who were living in an unreal world because they had fallen into lethargy woke up. It was a world populated by the lame, the blind and the dumb, but finally their eyes were opened again, their tongues were loosened and they were able to follow the way of truth. They could see everything with new eyes and they understood how deadly the food was that they had been feeding themselves on.

They knew how much that Father they had not wanted to listen to, loved them and finally they decided to attend the great banquet where he had been waiting for them for some time. He had suffered a lot seeing them delay so long, but His joy was so great at seeing them arrive in such great numbers that the wound in his heart was healed.

There was a huge celebration and the Father wanted to embrace personally each of his children. What emotion, what emotion in His gaze and His embrace so full of love! The tears were flowing freely and everyone's heart started beating with joy. Everyone was satisfying themselves fully with the delicious food, and they felt a great desire to make up for lost time.

Until then, the ship of their life had been at the mercy of the storm of selfishness, the hurricane of the passions and the waves of pleasure, and they had been thrown about here and there, often crashing into the sharp rocks. Now it was very clear to them that they had to turn the rudder towards the truth without ever again changing direction.

They understood why they had been dissatisfied: they had been created for other peaks, for the delicious fruits of love, peace and light, and they had preferred to go for putrid slime, letting themselves be intoxicated by the poisonous foods which they were offered from time to time. Finally, having tasted the delicious food of the banquet, they made a decision: they would be liberated from all the ballast of their selfishness which until now had suffocated them and weighed them down, stopping them from seeing and living; they would renounce the passions that had deceived them, the world's seductions and they would learn to fly in the true freedom of the sky of love.

This new people, made up of persons of every nation, every race and all ages, came together in a pact of unity. They said to one another: "We will always remain united in love and this will be our strength; we will not allow any division to weaken us. We will go through the world singing the wonders our Father has done for us. We will be ready to shed the last drop of the blood of soul and body so that Love will be loved by as many hearts as possible. We will sell everything in order to acquire the invaluable treasure of truth and never lose it again. We will walk the paths of the desert of humanity to quench the thirst of those in agony with the living water that is offered to us at the banquet of love and we will stay on the cross with the One who heals us, to heal the many wounds of our agonising and dying brothers and sisters. We will live so that those who are in darkness can see the light, so that those in anguish can savour peace, so that the dead can rise up.

"Yes, we will give witness to the world, to all who have never known love, that they are loved infinitely by the Love of loves. We will keep our eyes fixed on Heaven, so that each person we meet and look in the face, will know that Heaven exists. We will live together, putting everything in common, so that others, surprised by our love, can recognise that we are disciples of truth and feel attracted by true life. We will go through the whole world announcing the good news, binding the wounds of broken hearts, consoling the sick, proclaiming His infinite mercy. What does it matter if we have to give up our treasures, great or small, which until now have chained our hearts? What does it matter if we are persecuted and they think we are mad? In this crazy world we will be crazy with love."

Then I dreamed of this new people running through the streets of the world, taking fire where there is ice, colouring with fantastic embroideries of light darkness that had seemed impenetrable and irrigating with rain from heaven deserts that had been dry for centuries. I saw indescribably beautiful plants and flowers, I saw stars that had been extinguished for years reignited in the firmament of love, I saw disfigured lepers return to their original beauty, I saw many others reawaken from lethargy and many of the dead rise up again. They were all united with joy in the great dance of harmony and they were learning to fly in the Heaven of Love.

Then I saw lots of little towns of light rise up, spread all over the world like luminous floodlights pointing up to heaven, so that anyone being struck by those rays could be enchanted by the beauty of the firmament and decide to return and to sing with the other stars. They were little towns, yes, but their power to irradiate was immense, because the only law of these towns was love, and the rays of love cannot be stopped by anything or anyone. They were little towns where anyone who was wounded, in despair, destroyed or in agony could find refuge and be welcomed with the same love with which a mother embraces a sick child whom she hasn't seen for a long time. In these little towns I have seen many, and many finding rest, consolation and life and deciding to unite themselves, in their own time, to the pact of unity, so that others can discover the joy of living.

The first of these little towns was called Cittadella Cielo (heaven), because all those who lived there had taken the commitment to have, as their only law, the Word of Truth. They tried always to do the will of the Father, who is peace, joy, love and light, "on earth as it is in Heaven". The heavy burden of the personal story of those who came to live in Cittadella Cielo was of no importance. It didn't matter if, in the past, someone had stolen, sold drugs, been violent or committed any evil act. Each one had decided to throw their past, however terrible, into the infinite ocean of mercy, and as if by magic, they no longer felt crushed by it. All were committed to living the law of Heaven so that love could always reign in them and between them; a stupendous light illuminated the town drawing many others and rekindling in those who came to visit it, the irresistible desire for Heaven which has always been written on every human heart. Often, those who came to visit the town had terrible illnesses and very deep wounds; for this they needed the First Aid of Love and to spend some time in the little village Jeshua near the little town. In this little village, in fact, Jeshua (the One who heals) the world-famous and heavenly doctor, through his unique and meticulous art, eradicated every illness and healed every wound, including those thought to be incurable, which is a huge obstacle to the life of love.

In this little village everyone worked in an orderly manner and in harmony and, even though they felt tired because of the weakness caused by their past life, they wanted to learn finally, how to build, after having destroyed so much; what satisfaction, at the end of the day, to see the fruits of one's own work! At Jeshua there is no difference between those who arrived desperate and dying and those who, having been healed, wanted to make their own small contribution to help heal the wounds of the neediest of their brothers and sisters. Everyone had a lot to learn from the others and also plenty to give. The instruments of healing were very special: the "Gifts of the Paraclete"; the wounds were healed by the sweet balsam of the Spirit.

Once healed, having broken the chains of hedonism and selfishness with heavy hammer blows, those who had learnt to live according to the law of love were transferred from the Jeshua village to one of the many cottages in Cittadella Cielo.

All the inhabitants of the town were called "the little ones of joy", because having been healed by Jeshua they had learnt to see the beauty hidden behind everything and to be amazed by everything, just like children. They had also understood the mystery of wisdom hidden from the wise, but manifested to the little ones. Jeshua had performed a heart transplant on them: it had substituted the old heart of stone with a heart of flesh, overflowing with love and joy. This is why the least they could do was to sing to the world that, having suffered much, they had discovered a great treasure: the secret of joy. To acquire this treasure they had sold all their possessions, but now nothing and no one could take this joy from their hearts.

Then there were lots of cottages of Light where the Rainbow children lived. They were limpid and transparent like drops of water suspended between heaven and earth, constantly immersed in the light. The sun's rays, which shone in them and through them, showed the many shades of His beauty and coloured the earth with their harmony. The Rainbow children were all united in a marvellous dance which linked heaven to earth, forming a splendid bridge of colours. They shone in every moment with infinite colours of light and guarded in their hearts the great gifts in the other cottages.

Then there were the "little Micors brothers" who, after the deep emotion experienced at the Father's welcome having been away from him for so long, finally decided to go to His banquet, wanted to share their joy with the greatest possible number of people. They had arrived at the Father so dirty and muddy that they had been really afraid to come into his presence, but he welcomed them immediately into His warm embrace. In this way they had felt immersed in infinite mercy and had come back white as snow. In the midst of the great feast with the Father they had remembered many other brothers and sisters who had strayed far from the Father's house, and who were now dying of hunger and thirst, naked and imprisoned. So they had decided to run to them to feed them and to quench their thirst with the Father's delicious food and to remind them that they had been expected at the great banquet for some time and that the joy of their return would be immense.

In Cittadella Cielo there were also the cottages of Life where splendid mothers lived who, despite the many difficulties they experienced with their pregnancies, knew how to accept the great gift of life. Now their "little angels" were gladdening not only their mothers, but all the inhabitants of Cittadella Cielo.

In the Agape cottages lived all the children whose mothers had decided to abort them or who had not been able to keep them. On hearing the news that the "little ones of joy" would be happy to welcome these children, the mothers decided not to have an abortion but to entrust them to Cittadella Cielo. There were also lots of children who had been abandoned on the streets or sold into prostitution. All the inhabitants of the little town went often to the Agape cottages so that the children who had never known love could now live surrounded by great tenderness.

Then there were Mary's little ones who, captivated by the Flower of flowers of creation, had decided to become inebriated by that precious perfume so as to learn to put their roots in the heavenly garden, so that many others would be attracted to look at the things above. The Mother taught them to be little and to live constantly immersed in contemplation. Mary's little ones reminded everyone that only one thing is necessary: to stay at the Master's feet and listen to His Word which reveals the eternal mysteries.

In this very special little town there were also God's jesters and the apostles of love who, through art, shows, the mass media and other similar means went round the streets proclaiming out loud right up to the rooftops the wonders of love and the Good News. They had also created the "Beauty News" centre to contrast the use of the mass media to spread evil on behalf of the children of darkness with its use as a precious instrument to spread light and to uplift and edify many people.

In the little town there were many other wonderful things: the families of Nazareth, the little cenacles, the Emmanuelites, who went to the school of the grand Master to unmask the devious doctrines of false prophets and to inform with wisdom the different academic disciplines.

But the most important place was the house of the Treasure. There, people suffering from AIDS and other terminal illnesses lived as they prepared themselves for the moment when they would climb the marvellous luminous stairway linking the Cittadella to Paradise. The inhabitants of the little town went frequently to the house of the Treasure, because they knew that there were many important things to learn there and many valuable treasures to draw on.

After Cittadella Cielo many, many other little towns sprang up, and the number of persons who decided to join the new people became indeterminable. They were all flying from heaven to heaven, contemplating in endless wonder the ever new horizons of love.

I was sorry I had to wake up from my dream, but it seemed completely true to me, so much so that for an instant I hoped it was real. Now, my dear friend, all that remains for me to do is to share with you the joy that I felt in my heart because of this dream. You will say: "Yes, it's a beautiful dream, but like all dreams it's just a Utopia!" You are right, but great dreams help to change the course of history. And if by chance, my dream is also yours, we could start to come together, to enter and become part of that new people the Father is waiting for. Just think, if it really was our heavenly Father who put this dream in my heart and yours, we could genuinely hope one day to see it fulfilled and thank Him for having given us the chance to make our small contribution.

Maybe you will think: "So, you really are mad!" You're probably right, but anyway I have an indestructable certainty, because He gives me His Word: "What is impossible to men is possible to God." He knows how to realise even the most wonderful dreams. I hope I can meet you soon in the Heaven of love and explore with you, to our delight, His new horizons. And let's never be discouraged: everything is possible to God!

Epilogue

I bless you Chiara for all that the Lord has done through you and in you. I give thanks for this marvellous work of His sweet mercy.

The greatest need of the world today is to open to all, and to all those wounded by life, places of welcome that manifest the Father's mercy.

Places where they can be reborn to the life of God.

Places where those who are lacking in hope can receive Divine childhood, the new and eternal childhood!

Places where, through the offering of our wounds, the Spirit of God can be poured on to our poor, broken world.

Bless you Chiara, for these oases of tenderness for the poor and the little ones, that the Lord opens through your hands and through your heart.

Daniel-Ange
(founder of Jeunesse-Lumiere)

NEW HORIZONS

OUR HISTORY

The adventure of New Horizons began in 1991 when Chiara decided to make night-time visits to the central railway station in Rome (Stazione Termini) so that she could meet the many young people who are in very difficult situations and who have made the street their "home".

"When I began to go to the 'deserts' of our splendid Rome and to enter on tiptoe into the very painful stories of 'the people of the night', says Chiara, "I really did not think I would meet so many people who were desperate, alone, marginalized, begging to be loved, with their souls scarred by indifference, abandonment or violence. How many splendid people spoiled by evil, how many young people thirsting for the light but reduced by the seductions of the world and by the terrible blows of life to creatures with icy gazes and hearts of stone. How many young people in the full bloom of their youth gripped by a subtle sense of nausea, by a freezing existential emptiness, by a mortal anguish. How many desperate brothers and sisters with tears in their eyes have embraced me and asked, 'Please, Chiara, take me away from this hell!'… and what a suffering it was not to be able to find somewhere to take them!

"So the idea came to form a commun of welcome which would offer a pathw for healing the heart and for psychologi and spiritual regeneration."

In March 1994, Chiara opened the New Horizons community at Trigoria (Rom There, hundreds of young people com from the most extreme of experienc began to rebuild their lives throug therapeutic rehabilitation program designed by her. The immediate respo of the young people was surprisin encouraging. In May 1997 the Centre Formation and Welcome was opened Piglio, near Frosinone (south of Rome). was to become the headquarters of N Horizons. Between 1998 and 2007 furt communities of welcome were establis in Italy, as well as centres for formation reintegration, social projects and initiat for human development. In the year 2 the first activities abroad began, firs Brazil and then Bosnia.

> Chiara Amirante
> The first community of welcome at Trigo
> On the right: visit of Card. Tonini to Trigo

ardinal Ersilio Tonini

goria, on the furthest outskirts of Rome:
almost new, if poor, house. I was
elcomed there by a group of young
eople, almost all of whom were living
the streets. "Chiara will be here soon,"
d they rushed off to tell her of my
rival. I expected to see a serious looking, mature woman, but in fact it was a
l who is the picture of happiness who arrives. Then other young people arrived;
me of them had already consecrated their lives to God, others were preparing
do so, given the difficult and delicate mission which awaits them. This is where
e wonder begins. This new community has taken on the street as its field of
ission. I repeat: the **street**, which means the young people who populate it day
d night in a life of drugs, prostitution, alcohol, prison, violence. The story of this
ommunity began a few years ago at Stazione Termine in Rome where the
eatures that inhabited it seemed to form a people.

Chiara, like many others, saw this spectacle and was wounded to the heart.
e returned there many times until she took the decision: I will dedicate my life
these creatures! To decide is one thing, to go on and throw oneself into it and
are your life with them is quite another! New Horizons was born in this way. It
tracted first curiosity, then admiration, and finally wonder, and gradually the
umber of young people has grown who have seen, in this potentially risky
dertaking, a cause to which to devote their lives. The street is a merciless place,
here there is human degradation to make you shudder, heart-rending contortions,
within a relentless mechanism: *you become prostitute to be able to take drugs
d you take drugs to be able to become a prostitute.* It is a noose that is unforgiving.
t Chiara says she has discovered in these creatures a **divine spark**. Incredible
t true! Chiara is right to see behind the face of disintegrated creatures, a golden
lue, and to go in search of that gold buried beneath the detritus of vice. So it
ight, when that gold is found, to have a big celebration. Something else: Chiara
ays has a splendid, genuine smile… From our first meetings I understood that
ere was something out of the ordinary, precisely in the simplicity, the spontaneity,
what we call the Christian mystery: the abundance, the sublime simplicity and
verty; I understood very clearly that it was a work of the grace of God.

tracts from Cardinal Tonini's book *Splendor Veritatis* - *The Splendour of Truth* - and from his
eface to Chiara Amirante's book *Stazione Termini*).

WHO WE ARE

The aim of the New Horizons Community is to get involved wherever there is soc deprivation. So it offers solidarity and support to all who live in the most difficult situations. It carries out its activities fully aware of all the situations where there social deprivation and marginalisation, especially amongst the young. It offe specific, innovative activities and its own integrated programme of rehabilitati uniting psychological, spiritual and human elements.

It also encourages values of solidarity, sharing, spirituality and co-operation being essential for the fulfilment of the human person.

Chiara Amirante Fondatrice
Comunità NUOVI ORIZZONTI

WORKS AND PROJECTS

1 Residential Welcome Centres

29 Houses to welcome, support and orientate those in grave circumstances.
28 Formation houses for volunteers.
56 Families ready to welcome those in need.
27 Listening centres and telephone help lines which support over 100,000 people every year.

2. Centres providing Services

› **Prevention, sensitisation:** ;Every year arou 1,000,000 come to our many you people's gatherings: in schools, stree town centres, beaches, and throu concerts, interactive shows, meetir and round table discussions. Four or 1 times a year we organise street missic in each of these, which last ten days, meet some 35,000 people.

› **Communication and mass media:** (collaboration with the mass medic becoming more and more frequent c substantial: 545 television broadcasts which 119 are on RAI, the Italian natic TV network) and 1220 radio broadcc We print 15,000 copies of our quart magazine *Orizzonti News*. There are th web sites, various blogs… a numbe large events are organised.

› **Concerts and interactive shows:** Th have been numerous interactive sho and two musicals – *Stazione Termini* (*Nuovi Orizzonti* – which present problems of disaffected youth. They h proved to be very effective way:

nsitising the public and helping prevent ne problem.

ormation, cultural events, books and udio-visuals: Meetings, conventions, ducational packs aimed especially at oung people who are preparing to ecome volunteers, at social workers, arried and engaged couples, adolescents nd adults. 12 books have been published well as 4 music CDs, I DVD on the street issions and 1 multimedia CD on Project itadella Cielo.

ocial services and international co- peration: Development of the culture solidarity; activities of the social cretariat, finding volunteers in the most cially deprived places (prisons, hospitals, aces where there is poverty and egradation). Carrying out projects in ly and developing countries.

conomics and work: Promoting and ving value to the formative aspect of ork; planning work activities which help velop personal creativity; running ntres for help in getting back to work d social co-operatives.

rtistic expression: The expression and preciation of art, artistic creations such as paintings, icons, sculpture, craft work and design.

› **Spirituality and prayer:** There are currently 150 prayer groups supporting the Association.

3 Cittadella Cielo

4 Citadellas for welcome and formation are being developed around the world.

The New Horizons Community can count on the help of 6,500 people, of whom 5,500 are friends/supporters; more than 1,000 are collaborators, and 362 full-time volunteers. There are also thousands of sympathisers in Italy and abroad.

› Chiara at "On the Road to Damascus"
› Award of the Campidoglio Prize to Chiara Amirante 3 February, 2003
› Radio programme "Joyride"
› The "Roman Sport with New Horizons" event
› The "Joymix" show

PREVENTION

Members of the New Horizons Community are strongly committed to the wc of prevention, and numerous initiatives are undertaken to make young peop aware of problems such as drug dependence, alcoholism, anorexia and bulim and other forms of dependency and dysfunction which are violently afflicti young people. More than 5 million people have been met in Italy and abro through meetings, seminars, in schools, in prayer vigils, in city squares, on t streets and even on the beaches. There have been many television and rac broadcasts. 290,000 copies of the information bulletin have been distributed. well as 12 books published. Some young people of the community, The Jest of Love, have produced two musicals, "Stazione Termini" and "New Horizor with accompanying CDs. Various activities have been organized: a telephc

help-line, a social service secretariat, individ support counselling, formation groups, prevent meetings, day centres, street theatre, artistic c recreational activities, radio transmissions, theo workshops, formation courses for work on t streets…In addition support groups in numer schools have been established. Prevention c awareness-raising activities are carried out in schools every year.

› The musical "New Horizons"

› Moments of mission and evangelization

› Chiara meets young people at Agrigento in 2007

REET MISSIONS

ur or five times a year
treet Missions" are
ganized. These are
ecific initiatives with a
re team, assisted by a
ndred missionaries
any of whom come
m a life on the
eets), and numerous
lunteers who take
rt in one or other
oect of the mission.
nenever possible,
er communities,
ups and associations
e invited to
llaborate in the
ssion. Particularly
ot" areas of the city
e chosen, and for ten

consecutive days,
schools, bars, pubs,
discos, squares and
stations are "carpet-
bombed". Contact is
made with young
people through
individual
conversations, street
theatre, shows, musicals,
meetings, testimonies,
displays and workshops.
With their enthusiasm
and joy, the missionaries
succeed in arousing in
many young people
wonder, curiosity, hope
and often the decision
to change their life-style
and to embark on a
journey of self-
knowledge, personal
maturation and
recovery from situations
of dependency. This
maturation is achieved
by attending support

meetings or by
undertaking the
Association's
therapeutic
rehabilitation
programme. Many such
missions have been
carried out in Italy and
abroad.

INITIAL RECEPTION CENTRES

Young people encountered on the streets who want to enter a community are welcomed into a reception centre for a period of about one month. This time is necessary to strengthen the motivation to change life-style and, if required, for detoxification from drugs. Subsequently they are referred to a long-term residential centre.

The reception centres also carry out "work on the streets" and numerous other activities such as: telephone help-lines, individual counselling, prevention and awareness-raising meetings in schools, formation courses, artistic-recreational activities, spirituality groups, self-awareness groups and street missions.

LONG-TERM RESIDENTIAL CENTRES

On 13 May 1997, the residential centre at Piglio was opened in a beautiful Franciscan friary. Today the community houses around 70 young people

with problems relating to drug dependency, alcoholism, prostitution, AIDS or prison, and numerous volunteers who want to commit themselves to support those with such difficulties. The Piglio Community has become the "headquarters" of the Association. Since 1997 numerous communities of welcome have opened in Italy and abroad. Their specific characteristic is to be a large family open to all who want to have an experience of life renewed by Love. There are many young people in these communities who have a normal background but who have left their work and their home to live a strong community experience of solidarity. They undertake a formation course which equips them to accompany and sustain those with serious problems. Everyone, co-workers, leaders, young people from the streets, young people discovering their vocation, commit themselves to grow in the ART OF LOVING. They are sustained by a formation programme which develops self-knowledge and

interior healing, with an awareness that each person can be a gift for others.

› The community of welcome and formation at Piglio

› The community chapel at Piglio

HE NEW HORIZONS PROGRAMME

e therapeutic rehabilitation programme
ndertaken in the various long-term
sidential centres comprises five phases
self-knowledge:

Orientation

Behaviour — image

Self-awareness

Responsibility — decision-making

Reintegration — planning

> The Community at Montevarchi
> The Community at Pistoia

the **first phase**, work is done to
ngthen the young person's motivation
free themselves from the dynamics
the street and of dependency, so
o be able to undertake a demanding
rney towards a new life-style.

This is achieved through support
up meetings and individual interviews
dentify both the main problem areas
d appropriate solutions. Young people
h drug dependency problems are
companied and sustained as they
counter the numerous difficulties
ich the crisis of abstaining from
gs, alcohol or other dependencies
lves.

he **second phase**, young people
lcomed into the community are
ed to detach themselves from former
haviour and from attitudes of "the
eet". They are accompanied

individually on a journey where they
acquire personal responsibility and
awareness of their deviant behaviour.
The aim is to educate them to be able
to maintain commitments, take
responsibility and use their own creativity,
thus affirming their potential and unused
talents. Numerous ideas and tools for
improving behaviour and emotional
functioning are presented with the aim
of increasing self-control, authenticity,
interior freedom, a willingness to dialogue
with others and respect for oneself and
others. This work favours the acquisition
of a correct value system. If the second
phase is particularly important for
acquiring an initial awareness of their
unhealthy behaviour and attitudes, the

third phase of self-knowledge is a decisive moment for acquiring the necessary tools for changing them.

Various negatives behavioural pattens and dynamics, which have become entrenched over the years and have caused many problems for the individual, are clearly identified. Attention is focussed on what is needed to develop and own positive attitudes and behaviours.

Much space is given to group work and to formation, to sustain the young person in a journey of growth understood as:
- giving up destructive attitudes in order to adopt a positive and constructive vision of life;
- acquiring a healthy self-respect and rediscovering one's potential;
- growing awareness of the dynamics involved in feelings, emotions and mental processes;

- becoming reconciled to oneself one's past, to one's limits, to the differen between *the ideal and the real sel*
- ability to be oneself, free from condi ning and the fear of being judged;
- acquiring the ability to be pro-acti
- taking responsibility for one's d commitments and for relationships v others;
- growth in maturity and autonomy
- ability to choose and to judge;
- commitment and consistency in "here and now";
- ability to go beyond oneself to m others;
- dialogue and challenge in truth;
- growing awareness of one's inte spiritual dimension.

In the **fourth phase** of the program special attention is given to "responsib and decision-making". The young pe takes on positions of responsibilit work sectors and in the co-ordina and organization of the daily activ within the community. The commitm required in giving oneself to other teaching new arrivals what has b learned in the community and in ensu that everyone respects the rule particularly important for the prod of maturing and owning the r attitudes. In taking on responsibilit the younger members of the commu accompanying them as elder brot

The Community at Grottaferrata, Italy

Left

The Communities at Belpiano and Quixada in Brazil

reintegration. Finding a place in the world of work is a major element of this journey. As a first step the young person is given greater responsibility in work outside the community, and gradually participates in the social co-operative, as a way of assessing the level of maturity reached. The young person is then helped to rebuild their place in society. This involves looking for accommodation and work through which full personal autonomy can be reached.

The young person is supported as their progress in work, in the use of free time, in social reintegration, and in the area of affectivity is assessed in verification groups.

...d sisters and "guardian angels", the ...der members' reliability and ...mmitment grow. Taking on more ...ponsible roles, the young person ...ns to become more autonomous, to ...quire decision-making skills, and to ...ablish healthy relationships. In place ...fear and compromise, such ...ationships are based on authenticity, ...nesty and on managing one's ...otions and impulsivity. In this phase ...e young person can also become ...olved in prevention work (with schools ...d youth groups) and in work "on the ...eets".

...he **fifth phase** of the programme, ...young person is helped to develop ...skill of making plans for the future, ...part of the journey of social

Work methods/tools.
These are:

• individual counselling, through which the young person is guided, accompanied and sustained; therapy, and behavioural work;

• group work in the areas of self-knowledge, spirituality, sharing and the management of emotions;

• ergotherapy (work therapy), creativity, sport, relaxation techniques, time for meditation and personal and community prayer.

SOCIAL CO-OPERATIVES

Ergotherapy (work therapy)

In the New Horizons programme, work therapy is of primary importance, work being highly valued as an educational and formative tool. The community is above all a training ground for life, and it is precisely through work that each person's talents, capabilities, creative potential, self-discipline, responsibility and maturity are developed. There are numerous work sectors where the young people contribute on a rotational basis: icon workshop, kitchen garden, kitchen, laundry, production of musicals, administration, cleaning, building maintenance, carpentry, sweet-making, costume jewellery workshop, tapestry, handicraft, etc…

Social Co-operatives

Through the creativity and contribution of each member of the New Horiz family, new initiatives arise continually, such as the **"Blue Wings"** social co-operat

The aim of the social co-operatives is to give a concrete response to problem of the social and work reintegration of the young people who h completed the therapeutic programme. The co-operatives provide many servic gardening, production of garden objects, cleaning and building restoration w plastering, design and production of ceramics, terracotta, wood, and leat articles; production of information and prevention material; the organizatio celebrations (weddings, baptisms and other occasions).

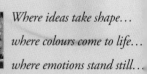

Where ideas take shape…
where colours come to life…
where emotions stand still…

www.preciousmomen

MISSIONS – Brazil

Quixadà

From early 2000 the New Horizons Community has been present in Brazil. The Mission is situated near Quixada, in north-east Brazil, in the State of Ceara. It is a town of great poverty where most of the dwellings are small and made of mud. There are many children who have made the street their home. Through the "Oasis of Peace" community, Providence gave us 100 hectares of land and consequently the diocese gave us the use of a further adjoining 300 hectares, including small lakes, where we are

building a "Little Town" (Cittadella Cielo).

Currently the Mission is made up of:
• a residential community of welcome for street children
• a reception community for young people
• two residential communities for adolescents and young people
• two centres for co-workers
• a centre for volunteer formation
• two family homes
• two reintegration centres.

In the town of Quixada itself, the following are operative:
• a day centre for receiving children ("The Perfect Joy House")
• a listening centre
• a social project "Coração" supporting 413 families living in poverty in the "favelas" (slums).

Fortaleza

At Fortaleza another splendid "Little Town" is being developed on 100 hectares of land given to Frei Hanz, founder of "Fazenda de Esperança". As well as New Horizons, 20 other Associations and Movements engaged in social projects are participating in this development.

Brazil
› The Quixadà Community
› The Fortaleza Community

MISSIONS – Bosnia

Thanks to Providence and the commitment of numerous volunteers who have worked with great dedication, the first of two Welcome Centres **Morning Star** has been established and work on the amphitheatre completed. The construction of the second centre is at a good stage. The two centres are situated on a splendid piece of land near the Church of Medjugorje which is visited by thousands of pilgrims each year from all parts of the world. Morning Star aims to be a Centre of welcome, formation and prayer for those wishing to dedicate a period of time to discernment in a setting of contemplation, and for members of the New Horizons Community who are preparing to leave to open new communities of welcome or missions, or to take on new tasks and responsibilities.

Since the summer of 2005 there has been a listening centre in the town. In the nearby locality of Capljina, in co-operation with the "Queen of Peace" Association, a village of welcome and formation **"Horizons of Peace"** has been developed. This comprises some ten centres on a 10-hectare piece of land and can provide residential welcome to more than 200 people.

Co-operation

Joint projects with the "Mary, Gate of Heaven" Association have been undertaken:
- a House of Welcome for 80 street children in Colombia
- a House of Welcome for 350 refugees in Albania
- a Community of Welcome for street children, a Centre for Professional Formation, and a school in Africa.

› Meetings with pilgrims the Morning Star Commur

› Youth Festival

› Horizons of Peace villag

SPIRITUALITY

Many members of the Association have wanted to consecrate their lives as a "Thank you of Love" to the Love of God. For this reason the "Private Association of the Faithful New Horizons" was constituted and approved by Cardinal Ruini on 10 March, 1997.

The general aim of the Association is the sanctity of the members who commit themselves to bringing Love to those who have not known Love, Life to those in death, the joy of the Resurrection to those who have lost Hope.

It is a lay consecration open to all states of life (celibacy, marriage, priesthood, religious life...), which gives special attention to the mystery of Jesus' descent into hell and his Resurrection.

CAMILLO
del Titolo di S. Agnese fuori le Mura
della Santa Romana Chiesa CARDINALE RUINI
Vicario Generale di Sua Santità
per la diocesi di Roma

Un gruppo di giovani fedeli animati da profondo spirito di carità al servizio dei più poveri ed abbandonati ha rivolto domanda a questo Vicariato perché venga riconosciuta nella Diocesi di Roma la Associazione privata di fedeli denominata "Nuovi Orizzonti".

I membri di tale Associazione intendono portare amore a chi non ha conosciuto l'Amore, Luce a chi è nelle tenebre, Vita a chi è nella morte e si consacrano a Dio nella certezza che la loro vita potrà diventare canale della Sua potenza e della Sua misericordia.

Apprezzata l'intensa e feconda opera di apostolato che l'Associazione svolge

DECRETO

l'Associazione "NUOVI ORIZZONTI", retta dall'allegato statuto, è riconosciuta come Associazione privata di fedeli nella Diocesi di Roma a norma del can. 299 §3.

Esorto dunque tutti gli appartenenti a detta Associazione di vivere la dimensione autentica della carità secondo lo spirito della fondatrice Chiara Amirante e quanto espresso dallo statuto.

Dato a Roma dal Palazzo Lateranense, il giorno 4 marzo A.D. 1997.

Prot. n. 255/97

SECRETARIA STATUS

Il Sommo Pontefice
GIOVANNI PAOLO II

ha nominato per un quinquennio Consultore del Pontificio Consiglio della Pastorale per i Migranti l'Illustrissima Signorina

Dott.ssa CHIARA AMIRANTE

Tanto si partecipa allo stesso Illustrissima Signorina Amirante per sua opportuna conoscenza e norma.

Dal Vaticano, 18 Luglio 2004.

Segretario di Stato

SPIRITUALITY

There are currently 362 consecrated members of the Association; they make promises of poverty, chastity, obedience and… joy. The specific vocation of each consecrated member is to bear witness that Christ came to give us the "fullness of his joy" (Jn 17:13): "Remain in my love, if you keep my commandments you will remain in my love…I have told you these things so that my joy may be in you and your joy be complete" (Jn 15: 8-11).

THE KNIGHTS OF THE LIGHT
These are people of the New Horizons Community (or of other movements, associations and ecclesial communities) who commit themselves

to live the Word of God with radicalit to announce the Good News to mar and to take the revolution of the Gospel into the world.

CASA EMMANUEL
This is the house for young people w want to discern their vocation and fc formation to the priesthood, at the service of the specific charism of the New Horizons Community. As well as undertaking theology courses, the young people of Casa Emmanuel follow an intense programme with many moments of personal and community prayer, and groups for formation, self-knowledge, sharing and spirituality. Pastoral work is undertaken in many spheres, with particular attention given to evangelization and to "street work".

› Sala Nervi, Chiara at the meeting of Pope John Paul II with young people -19

› Meeting with Pope Benedict XVI — May 2006

› Chiara with consecrated members, Pentecost 2007

THE LITTLE TOWN "CITTADELLA CIELO" PROJECT

his project aims to establish Little Towns cittadelle") of welcome and formation here the reconstruction of the human erson and healing from the many ynamics of dependency are undertaken. ey are places where one learns to e according to the Law of Heaven, e Love which Christ came to teach , and prepares to establish in Italy and road the following:

ntres of welcome and support for life: all villages for street children; family uses; centres for listening, telephone lplines, support groups, street teams; ntres for volunteer formation; social -operatives; centres for reintegration o the world of work; shows, broadcasts, idarity concerts, initiatives for prevention d awareness-raising; self-knowledge urses; formation courses for those rking in the social field and for ucators; street missions; spirituality ntres; projects in developing countries; atever else the imagination suggests reply to the cry of suffering of those serious difficulties.

r dream is a small town, open to lcome the poor, the little ones, the ast", where all who feel alone, rginalized, without hope, can rediscover joy of feeling welcomed, supported, ed.

The "Cittadella" will also be a centre for co-operation between the many groups throughout Italy working with social problems and deviancy, and will be a "pilot project" repeatable in other parts of Italy and abroad.

The Little Town "Cittadella Cielo" Project includes:

1) Houses of welcome for volunteers in formation who will be committed in the areas of work, therapy and organization, in numerous formation courses and in

› The first development stage of "Cittadella Cielo", Frosinone, Italy.

social initiatives of prevention, support and guidance. They will also maintain links with the surrounding area and with the public services and be involved in "street work", awareness-raising and prevention.

2) A small village for welcoming life, offering residential support to young single mothers and children in difficulty; "Agape Communities" which welcome abandoned children.

3) A Study and Communication Centre for the production of information material in co-operation with the mass-media, particular attention being given to issues of prevention.

4) A formation centre for artists whi⟨ will help them use their personal talen to produce artistic events (music, theat films, painting, design, etc.) of soc significance and effective in the preventi of social problems.

5) A formation centre for those worki on the streets.

6) A centre for offering immediate supp for those in situations of serious difficu to accompany them towards t appropriate support structure of t New Horizons Community or oth Associations.

7) A centre of spirituality and praye

8) A centre to welcome and supp young people with AIDS and termi illnesses.

9) Street teams who will work in the "h areas, in schools, in prisons, and in t places where young people gathe

10) Social co-operatives to create w opportunities for the disadvantage

11) Centres for listening and guidan⟨

12) Support groups.

13) A multi-functional youth centre

› The "Horizons of Peace" Cittadella, Bosnia.

PERHAPS NOT EVERYONE KNOWS THAT…

According to Unicef statistics there are more than 100 million young people living in the streets who are victims of violence, abuse, exploitation of every kind, and the phenomenon is growing almost everywhere. It is a real social emergency. According to a report of the Commission for Human Rights, 150 million female children and 73 million male children were abused through forced sexual relationships in 2005. It is calculated that there are currently 70,000 websites containing paedo-pornographic material. According to the World Health Organization, every year an average of 53 million abortions are carried out. Statistics from the United Nations Office on Drugs and Crime report that 3% of the world's population abuses drugs. WHO statistics say that alcohol abuse is the cause of 60% of accidents, 9% of disabilities, 41% of homicides, and 10% of illnesses. According to a survey carried out in more than two hundred schools Italy, 80% of adolescents show at least one of the worrying symptoms which characterize the world of young people: alcohol abuse, use of drugs (above all cannabis, and one in four adolescents uses synthetic drugs e.g. ecstasy etc.), sexual deviancy, anorexia and bulimia, depressive states, serious family problems…and there is an almost total lack of intervention. It is estimated that in Italy about 7 million people consume alcohol at a level which puts them at risk; 8-10% of girls suffer from anorexia and bulimia, and 72% of women are victims of violence. In addition there has been a notable increase in "slave prostitution", in sex tourism, paedophilia (the violence and outrages connected to this terrible traffic are startling). We want to commit ourselves fully to working together with others to respond as much as possible to the terrible cry of too many of our sisters and brothers which continually challenges us and "compels" us to put ourselves on the front line!

THERE ARE MILLIONS OF PEOPLE THROUGHOUT THE WORLD WHO DIE IN TRULY DRAMATIC SITUATIONS. NOT TO DO EVERYTHING POSSIBLE TO PREVENT THESE DEATHS IS A FAILURE TO HELP. A LITTLE LOVE CAN SAVE A LIFE!! YOUR CONTRIBUTION IS VERY PRECIOUS. THANK YOU FOR WHATEVER YOU CAN MANAGE TO DO.

We want to commit ourselves fully and work together with others to respond to the terrible cry of too many of our sisters and brothers.
Our contribution is very precious!

HOW TO SUPPORT US

Central Office in Piglio (FR):
Telephone 0039 0775 502353
Email: piglio@nuoviorizzonti-onlus.com

Silvia Piasentini
DIRECTOR OF COMMUNICATIONS
Email: Silvia.p@nuoviorizzonti-onlus.com

• **TO SUPPORT OUR PROJECTS** •

• **Pay into the following bank account:**
Ass. Nuovi Orizzonti
UNICREDIT - Banca di Roma - Filiale di Piglio
Iban IT49E0300274520000400404638
Swift BROMITR1472

Ass. Nuovi Orizzonti Onlus
UNICREDIT - Banca di Roma - Filiale di Piglio
Iban IT98F0300274520000400406641
Swift BROMITR1472
(donations tax-deductible)

• **Support the "Cittadella Cielo" project:**
Pay into one of the accounts above,
specifying "for project Cittadella Cielo"

Join adoptions at a distance in Brazil:
Adoptions at a distanc
26 Euros per month or 312 Euros per year with
direct debit to the following account

Ass. di Vol. Nuovi Orizzonti On
UNICREDIT - Banca di Roma, Agenzia di Pig
Iban IT81W0300274520000400417€
Swift BROMITR14

Specify adoptions at a distance or missionary
a distance, plus your address (donatic
tax-deductibl

When you subscribe to the adoption schen
and/or for further information, conta

Adoptions Offi
Tel. 335 7052428 (or 0775 5023
Email: ufficioadozioni@nuoviorizzonti-onlus.cc

• **Pray for us**
• **Form small prayer cenacles**
email: cenacoli@nuoviorizzonti-onlus.com
• **Offer your talents and ideas**
• **Join one of the work groups**
• **Make use of the services of our social co-opera**
"Ali Blu".

FOR FURTHER INFORMATION

www.nuoviorizzonti-onlus.com
www.cittadellacielo.com
www.cavalieridellaluce.net

BUY OUR PUBLICATIONS

- **Stazione Termini**, Chiara's dialogue with the young people at the station. 1994 (16th edition) Città Nuova
- **Nuovi Orizzonti***, Chiara's autobiography and the story of the Community. 1997 (5th edition) Città Nuova
- **Il regno della gioia**, a parable on "The Journey of Life". 2000 (5th edition) Shalom
- **Alzati e rivestiti di luce**, Chiara's meditations for the start of each day. 2005 (3rd edition) Città Nuova
- **Gioia Piena**, exercises to help you never be sad. 2007 (1st edition) Città Nuova

New Horizons, Chiara's autobiography and the story of the Community. 2009 (1st edition) New City

here is also a
COLLECTION OF TITLES REGARDING
THE NEW HORIZONS SPIRITUALITY
roduced together with the publishers OCD:

Pregare è amare: spiritual exercises
th edition) 2005
Il Paradiso non può attendere: live the joy
heaven now (3rd edition) 2006
Il sole nell'abisso: colour the darkness of
e world with joy. (1st edition) 2006
Fuoco dal cielo: fly with the wings of the
ly Spirit (1st edition) 2007
Il prodigio che è in te: (1st edition) 2008

CD

Francesco Picollo's CD Gocce di cielo

Francesco Picollo's CD Il suono dell'Anima

Francesco Picollo's CD which includes songs from the musical Nuovi Orizzonti

Music for meditation composed and arranged by Marco Guadin

Chiara Amirante's meditations on CD and audio cassette

SOME ADDRESSES

IN ITALY

Piglio (FR): Sede Centrale -Via Prenestina 95, 03010 Piglio (FR) - Tel/Fax 0775 502353
E-mai:l piglio@nuoviorizzonti-onlus.com

• **Piglio: Casa di formazione al presbiterato Emmanuel** 339 3281385

• **Roma:** centro di prima accoglienza, **"Centro Arcobaleno":** Via Portoferraio 9,00182 Roma (RM) - Tel/Fax 0670305159 / 0670391267
E-mail arcobaleno@nuoviorizzonti-onlus.com

• **Roma:** centro di evangelizzazione , P.le Clodio, 00100 Roma (RM)

• **Marino (RM): "Casa Gioia"**, Pza Garibaldi 8, 00047 Marino (RM) - Tel/Fax 06 93803113
E-mail: casagioia@nuoviorizzonti-onlus.com

• **Marino (RM): casa Piccole Sorelle di Gesù Risorto**, Pzza Garibaldi 37,00047 Marino (RM), Tel /Fax 06 93803113

• **Grottaferrata:** Via colle delle Ginestre 69, 00046 Grottaferrata- Tel/Fax 06 94315460
E-mail: grottaferrata.nuoviorizzonti@gmail.com

• **Frosinone: "Rejoyce"** centro di ascolto tel 331 9253951
msn: nuoviorizzontipiglio@hotmail.it
skype: nuoviorizzontipiglio

• **Guidonia (RM):** Comunità Città della Gioia, via delle Molette fnc 00012 Guidonia Tel 0774 304158
E-mail: guidoniai@nuoviorizzonti-onlus.com

• **Montevarchi:** centro di accoglienza ,centro di reinserimento **"casa Alleluja"** Via Pestello Campagna 7, 52025 Montevarchi (AR), Tel 055 984819, Fax 055 9850807
E-mail: montevarchi@nuoviorizzonti-onlus.com

• **Padova:** casa Magnificat, Via Tre garofani, 65/67, 35124, Padova (PD) Tel 049 605147
E-mail: padova@nuoviorizzonti-onlus.com

• **Pistoia:** centro di accoglienza **"casa Francesco"**, centro di reinserimento **"ca S.Giuseppe"**, Via Castellina 20,51030 Casa del Monte (PT) Tel/Fax 0572 618067
E-mail: pistoia@nuoviorizzonti-onlus.com

• **CEI (TN):** centro di formazione e di evangelizzazione **"Ass. trentina Nuovi Orizza onlus"**, località Bellaria di CEI 38060, Villalagar (TN) Tel 0464 800002 Fax 0464 800291
E-mail: trento@nuoviorizzonti-onlus.com

• **Rovereto (TN):** centro di ascolto **"ca Isacco"** , Tel 348 2205172

• **Ischia (NA): "centro Giovanni Paolo II"** Via Purgatorio snc, 80075 Forio d'Ischia (N Tel 081 998813
E-mail: ischia@nuoviorizzonti-onlus.com

ABROAD
• **Medjugorje: "centro Stella del Mattino** (Bosnia Herzegovina): Tel 00387 634335 Fax 00387 36651957
E-mail medjugorje@nuoviorizzonti-onlus.c

• **Brazil: Cittadella Cielo Rainha Do Sertã** Associacao Novos Horizontes Estrada Juatama, s/n° Caixa Postal 01 Serra du Uru 63.900.000 Quixadà (Cearà) Tel. 0055/88.99.68.17.42
E-mail novoshorizontesrainha@gmail.co

• **Brazil: Cidadela Ceu** – Associacao No Horizontes Condominio Espiritual – Uirap (CEU) (In collab. con Fazenda de Esperan Casa do menor, Shalom, Cancionas Nova Av. Alberto Craveiro n. 2222, Castelo Fortaleza – 60.860.000 Tel.0055/85.32.89.4
E-mail: novohorizontesceu@gmail.com

ONLY LOVE

In my journey in the world of the street I have gathered thousands of tears which I still keep as a precious treasure in my heart; I have listened to the silent cries of the people of the night; I have entered on tiptoe into the deserts of souls thirsting for love; I have seen an incredible number of hands held out in desperate search of help and... much, too much indifference! I have seen girls of a tender age marked with scars and cigarette burns, forced in full view of everybody into the most shameful of slaveries. I have listened to the weeping of beautiful young people reduced to "living deaths" in the illusion of an artificial paradise which has stolen their souls; I have embraced wonderful children abandoned on the streets, who were begging for just a bit of tenderness... I have felt the cry of this innumerable people of the small and the poor pierce my heart and I asked myself: "What can I do?" I then heard another cry... a cry of Love!! The cry of a crucified God who took death upon himself to give us Life, anguish to give us Peace, each of our sufferings to fill them with his infinite Love... The cry of the Man-God who today still passes through the deserts of the world repeating to us: "Love one another as I have loved you!" And in that cry I found the answer.

Yes, only Love can dismantle the walls of indifference which imprison the soul in a mortal solitude.

Only Love can destroy the anguish of hearts turned into stone by hatred and violence. Only Love can give back hope to those who, struck by the terrible blows of life, are prostrate in desperation. Only Love can make the Joy of living spring up in the deserts of humanity.

It is stupendous to discover the new horizons which Love reveals continually, and we want to live this adventure together with all who feel a deep "thirst for Heaven". The horizon is the place where earth and sky meet, and the New Horizon Communities are born precisely to enable all who feel desperate, thanks to Love, to rediscover joy and to live a bit of Heaven already on this earth.

We need your help too in bringing to the world the revolution of love!

Chiara Amirante